Edward Bond: A Critical Study

Edward Bond: A Critical Study

Peter Billingham

First published 2013 by
PALGRAVE MACMILLAN

Palgrave Macmillan in the UK is an imprint of Macmillan Publishers Limited, registered in England, company number 785998, of Houndmills, Basingstoke, Hampshire RG21 6XS.

Palgrave Macmillan in the US is a division of St Martin's Press LLC, 175 Fifth Avenue, New York, NY 10010.

Palgrave Macmillan is the global academic imprint of the above companies and has companies and representatives throughout the world.

Palgrave® and Macmillan® are registered trademarks in the United States, the United Kingdom, Europe and other countries.

ISBN 978–0–230–36739–5

This book is printed on paper suitable for recycling and made from fully managed and sustained forest sources. Logging, pulping and manufacturing processes are expected to conform to the environmental regulations of the country of origin.

A catalogue record for this book is available from the British Library.

A catalog record for this book is available from the Library of Congress.

Typeset by MPS Limited, Chennai, India.

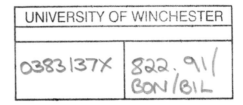

*To my parents Grace and Ernie, both in rest
at the inland sea*

Contents

List of Illustrations

Acknowledgements

Researching and writing this book has been a massive endeavour in a number of ways, but one that I have found immensely stimulating and rewarding. I would like to take this opportunity firstly to thank the many friends and professional colleagues who have contributed support and interest throughout the preparation and writing of this book.

Amongst my colleagues at the University of Winchester I would like to thank Professor Anthony Dean, Dean of the Faculty of Arts, and Dr Inga Bryden, Faculty Director of Research and Knowledge Exchange, for their supporting of teaching-relief for me during the final, demanding months of completing the original manuscript. I would also like to express thanks and appreciation to a wider circle of friends and colleagues for their friendship and professional support: Professor John Bull, Professor Tony Howard, Dr Graham Saunders, Tony Coult, Dr Cesar Villa, Dr Kate Katafiasz and Dr Stevie Simkin.

I am also extremely grateful to Sean Holmes (Artistic Director, The Lyric Theatre, Hammersmith) and Chris Cooper (Artistic Director, Big Brum Theatre in Education company) for their very generous giving of time and support to this project.

Formal acknowledgements to the following for permission to use production photographs of Bond's plays: Simon Kane (*Saved*), Chris Cooper (*The Under Room, At the Inland Sea, The Balancing Act*) and Corin Evans Pritchard (*The Children*).

I also want to express my thanks and appreciation to Paula Kennedy for commissioning this book and Sacha Lake for her help and support. My sincere thanks also to Monica Kendall for her priceless support and expertise in the final editing process. Finally I must thank Sally Ashworth for her expertise and commitment in compiling the index.

I would like to think a former colleague and friend from the University of Portsmouth, John Stanton, for his invaluable contribution to my production of *At the Inland Sea*. I would also like to acknowledge the talent and commitment of the student casts of *Red Black and Ignorant* (Bath Spa University, 2004), *At the Inland Sea* (University of

Portsmouth, 2006), *Passion* and *The Children* (University of Winchester, 2011 and 2012). I have very much enjoyed directing those young actors in Bond's plays.

The ever present love, support and good fun shown by my family have as always been priceless: Eve, Chris, Millie and Poppy, Tom, Sally, Leo and Josh, and William, Ruth and Simon. Most importantly, Marilyn's patience and understanding during a demanding creative process and her belief in the book and its author are deeply valued and appreciated.

The ideas and interpretations offered in this book are mine alone, and should not be taken in any way to represent those of Edward Bond himself.

List of Abbreviations

AIS   *At the Inland Sea: A Play for Young People* (London: Methuen, 1997)

B   *Bingo*, in *Plays: 3* (*Bingo, The Fool, The Woman, Stone*) (London: Methuen Drama, 1987)

C   *Chair*, in *The Under Room*, in *Plays: 8* (*Born, People, Chair, Existence, The Under Room*) (London: Methuen Drama, 2006)

CTFC   *The Crime of the Twenty-First Century*, in *Plays: 7* (*Olly's Prison, Coffee, The Crime of the Twenty-First Century, The Swing, Derek, Fables and Stories*) (London: Methuen Drama, 2003)

F   *The Fool*, in *Plays: 3* (*Bingo, The Fool, The Woman, Stone*) (London: Methuen Drama, 1987)

HIN   *Have I None*, in *The Chair Plays* (*Have I None, The Under Room, Chair*) (London: Methuen Drama, 2012)

I   *Innocence*, in *Plays: 9* (*Innocence, The Balancing Act, Tune, A Window, The Edge*) (London: Methuen Drama, 2011)

L   *Lear*, in *Plays: 2* (*Lear, The Sea, Narrow Road to the Deep North, Black Mass, Passion*) (London: Methuen Drama, 1978)

PW   *The Pope's Wedding*, in *Plays: 1* (*Saved, Early Morning, The Pope's Wedding*) (London: Methuen Drama, 1977)

R   *Restoration*, in *Plays: 4* (*The Worlds, The Activist Papers, Restoration, Summer*) (London: Methuen Drama, 1992)

T   *Tune*, in *Plays: 9* (*Innocence, The Balancing Act, Tune, A Window, The Edge*) (London: Methuen Drama, 2011)

TC   *The Children*, in *The Children* and *Have I None* (London: Methuen Drama, 2000)

UR   *The Under Room*, in *Plays: 8* (*Born, People, Chair, Existence, The Under Room*) (London: Methuen Drama, 2006)

W   *The Worlds*, in *Plays: 4* (*The Worlds, The Activist Papers, Restoration, Summer*) (London: Methuen Drama, 1992)

Introduction
Wearing Dead Men's Clothes: Addressing the Past, Re-dressing the Future

Edward Bond is one of the major British dramatists of the post-war period. He remains arguably one of the most provocative voices in British theatre in the twentieth and twenty-first centuries. An integral element in helping to assess the value and status of his writing over the past half-century is the wider international context in which both his earlier major works and more recent plays are produced. From the early to mid 1990s especially, his plays have received a substantial critical reception in France. His plays have also been successfully produced in Germany, Italy and more recently Canada.

In addition to his defining role as a dramatist he is also a cultural theoretician, essayist and poet. His career dates back to the first professional performance of his play *The Pope's Wedding* (1962). Since then his work has been characterised by a rigorously rational, materialist view of humanness, society and culture. This is not a simplistic or reductive cultural materialism. This book explores and discusses how Bond has evolved over the past 50 years (1962–2012) an interrogative, radically self-reflexive, muscular poetic materialism. It informs and characterises all of his work.

'Let us now be serious and for a start change everything'

(The title of this section is a quote by Edward Bond in a programme note for a 2010 production of his rewritten version of *Red Black and Ignorant*.)

I want to turn next to a broadly chronological overview of Bond's life and work. I am grateful to all those who have researched and published earlier studies of Bond. Early landmarks were notably Hay and Roberts (1980) and Coult (1977). Much of the early to mid-career biographical information regarding Bond was established in those earlier studies. I am grateful to have been able to draw on those two studies for that purpose. This biographical context helps to provide a useful framework in which to discuss those other plays by Bond outside the generic groupings I have used in Chapters 1 and 2.

Bond's early opportunities as a playwright and the rapid rise of his reputation are inescapably bound up with a crucial period in post-war British theatre. This was during the mid-to-late 1950s in which the English Stage Company (ESC) emerged at the Royal Court Theatre, London, under the initial leadership of the director and actor George Devine. There was also simultaneously the emergence of a robust, popular people's political theatre led by Joan Littlewood at the Theatre Royal, Stratford East. This period of the 'New Wave' in British theatre might usefully be viewed as starting with the Royal Court's production of John Osborne's *Look Back in Anger* in 1956 and closing with Littlewood's *Oh! What a Lovely War!* in 1963. William Gaskill's seminal Royal Court production of Bond's *Saved* in 1965 marked a high-water point in this first decade of new playwriting. It also embodied a profound renewal in British directing and production for the stage. This project, the product of a new generation of writers (some of them, like Bond and Arnold Wesker, from working-class backgrounds) and directors (such as Gaskill, Tony Richardson, Lindsay Anderson and others) grew out of the economic optimism of the period. This also facilitated the building of new theatres. The election of Harold Wilson's Labour government in 1964 hardly heralded a radical alternative to the previous 13 years of Conservative rule, but this period nevertheless saw writers on the Left such as Bond, Wesker and John Arden (along with Osborne, whose political position at that time would have been viewed as liberal-left) finding stages and audiences for their work.

Edward Bond was born on 18 July 1934 in Holloway, North London, one of four children. His father, Gaston Cyril Bond, was a farm labourer and later an auto painter in a garage; his mother, Florence Kate (née Baker), remained at home bringing up the family. Bond describes his upbringing as 'Lower working class but not London working class. My parents had come up to London during the depression because they couldn't get work on the land. My father had been a labourer in Suffolk and he did various kinds of labouring jobs when he was in London' (Bond qtd in Roberts, 1985, p. 7).

As a direct consequence of the German bombing of the capital, in 1940 the six-year-old Bond was evacuated to Cornwall and subsequently to Ely in Cambridgeshire, East Anglia, where he lived with his grandparents. In 1944 he returned to London and attended Crouch End Secondary Modern School, as he was not considered academically able enough to take the select Grammar schools' entrance examination (commonly known as the Eleven-Plus). He later observed: 'That was the making of me, of course. You see, after that nobody takes you seriously. The conditioning process stops. Once you let them send you to grammar school and university, you're ruined' (Bond qtd in Hay and Roberts, 1980, p. 7).

In 1948, at the age of 14 and in his penultimate year at school, he attended a production of *Macbeth* produced by the last of the great touring British actor-managers, Donald Wolfit. Wolfit was known for the epic scale, grandeur and intense emotional range of his acting. The young Bond was indelibly impressed, calling the event, 'The first thing that made sense of my life for me ... naturally, when I wrote, I wrote for the theatre' (Bond qtd in Hay and Roberts, 1980, p. 7). His strong sense of engagement with theatre and performance was also enhanced by regular visits to the music hall where his sister worked.

After leaving school at 15 without formal qualifications, Bond worked as an office junior before being called up in 1953, at the age of 19, to fulfil his compulsory two years of military national service. He served in the army as an infantryman and wrote his first serious work (the first part of a novel, left unfinished) while stationed in Vienna. Bond's traumatic experience of military culture and practice was a key event in his life; he recalled, 'I was in the infantry, cut off from the outside world for six weeks – degrading, hair cut, strange clothes, shouted at, screamed at. We were turned into automata' (Bond qtd in Hay and Roberts, 1980, p. 7). This dehumanising and alienating conditioning of the human being into a robotic 'automaton', programmed to obey orders, hate and kill for the monarch and the state is a recurring theme in Bond's work.

In his Author's Preface to *Lear*, Bond writes, 'I write about violence as naturally as Jane Austen wrote about manners' (Bond, 1978, p. 3). For Bond violence always has a specific material and ideological site. This is one in which violence is frequently sanctioned by the monarchy or the state as a means and expression of power and control, and the crushing of resistance to the political hierarchy.

On completing his national service, Bond began to write plays. He had written about 15 and had unsuccessfully submitted some of them to the BBC. In 1958 he was invited to join one of the writers' groups established at the Royal Court Theatre by Gaskill, at that time an assistant director to Devine. In this context he also became a regular play reader for the theatre. He remembered later how useful the experience was: 'In this group we practised improvisation and a few elementary acting exercises. The group was always run by directors and not writers. This was good because it made the members aware of the plastic, visual nature of theatre' (Bond qtd in Roberts, 1985, p. 7). In the context of a jaded post-war British theatre that, with rare exceptions, was controlled and owned by a commercial, West End mentality, Devine's aims, while not revolutionary, offered a thoughtful and challenging form of theatre. This reflected a time of significant social, political and cultural change.

On 9 December 1962 Bond's first produced play for the Royal Court Theatre, *The Pope's Wedding*, was staged as a single performance as part of a season that company instituted called 'Sunday Night Productions without Decor'. It was directed by Keith Johnston in what might now more usually be described as a platform performance or rehearsed reading. These Sunday evening productions provided new, untested writers such as Bond with an opportunity to have their dramatic voices heard and nurtured through the fundamentals of performance.

Bond's play is set in East Anglia, where he had spent some of his formative years during the wartime evacuation. His antecedents were also from that region. The characters are the rural working class, living precariously on subsistence wages, constantly needing to subsidise their social lives and routines through borrowing cigarettes or the price of the next pint of beer from each other. The characters speak with an acutely observed East Anglian dialect. However, unlike Wesker's play from the same period (*Roots*, 1959), Bond's play, for all of its equivalent geographical location and class setting, is not a piece of left-wing social realism. Indeed, and critically, Bond's work is not engaged in a realist generic discourse in any constraining sense. What is a common factor in both of these plays is that those rural farming communities in the east of England are characteristically isolated, creating a powerful sense of entrapped and marginalised lives.

The Pope's Wedding focuses upon the central dramatic narrative of Scopey, a young farm labourer. This character initially embodies his class contemporaries' prejudice and violence towards an old hermit, Alen, who lives on the edge of the village – on the margins in both a literal and also, crucially, a metaphorical and ideological sense. Scopey has married Pat in the early stages of the play. She is of the same generation and class as him. Complying with a promise made by her late mother to take care of Alen, Pat has been visiting the old man and cleaning and cooking for him. While at first Scopey is frustrated with the unpaid time and attention that Pat devotes to Alen, almost irresistibly he begins to assume her role of carer to this estranged, uncommunicative, older man. This relationship evolves on a deepening sense of Scopey's problematic identification and empathy towards Alen. It is ultimately, bleakly realised when Scopey, having murdered Alen for profoundly inexplicable reasons, assumes his clothes and persona. It's as if a tragic ontological and existential act of transference has taken place. Scopey seeks to 'become' the 'other': an aspiration and displaced desire as impossible as the contradiction inherent in the play's title.

Earlier in the play, other youths from the village have regularly and violently visited the old man's house. The ideological function of classical dramatic tragedy in Athens defined Fate as having an innate inevitability initiated by the gods. It frequently achieved its ends through violent means. This concept of a preordained Fate provided a way in which the ideological contradiction between a socially and culturally advanced society, dependent on a slave economy, could be 'disguised'. The gods and Fate facilitate a rationale and an ideological sleight of hand to signify and paradoxically conceal economic surplus and its consequent cultural capital. The inevitability of inequality is subsequently sanctioned. However, the violence enacted by Scopey is no more 'inevitable' in its action and causes than the continuing military engagement of British and American troops in foreign theatres of war. As Bond wrote in 1972:

> The pope's wedding is an impossible ceremony – Scopey's asking for an invitation for something that isn't going to happen, that *can't* happen ... what I wanted to do was to try and get inside the

image, and see what it was all about. This is what Scopey does in the play, and in the end he kills a man and wears his clothes in order to find out. And of course there's nothing there. (Bond qtd in Roberts, 1985, p. 14)

For Bond, violence is the *a priori* of human suffering and exploitation, though he clearly distinguishes the function of violence-as-instinct within the natural predatory life cycles of the animal world from the violence exhibited and institutionalised by humans and their societies.

The Pope's Wedding, with its distinctive treatment of its themes of an alienated, rural working class, helped to establish Bond's reputation as an important young writer. It also marked the beginnings of a changing critical response to his work: the initial perplexity and ultimately moral outrage about Bond's use of violence. Additionally, the play provides evidence of the seminal presence of Bond's later, developed thinking about both politics and theatre in his earliest work. This thinking is characterised by a profound exploration of important issues of 'being' and 'knowing' and their related discourse. At the risk of reductive summary, in the complex web of Scopey's motives and actions, Kant is already emerging in the early 1960s as significantly as Marx in Bond's treatment of class alienation and existential angst. However, for Bond, the construct of individual subjectivity and interior motivation is both problematic and, at best, only a symptom of the wider social, cultural and political influences that define human beings.

Throughout his career, Bond has continually pondered on the nature, causes and function of violence in society. One of the most unforgettable and iconic images and events in post-war British theatre and twentieth-century theatre as a whole is realised in his next play, *Saved* (1965), in the stoning to death of a baby in a pram in a public park by a group of young men. This unsurprisingly shocked contemporary reviewers and audiences. There were angry disturbances on its opening night. For Bond, violence is always principally a product and symptom of corrupt and exploitative social organisations. Therefore, within the dramatic site of the park in *Saved*, the violence may be viewed and analysed from multiple but complicit standpoints. On one level it is a savagely premeditated demonstration of socially gendered codes of masculinity-as-violence. Simultaneously, this public exhibition of violence also reflects and expresses the wider meta-narratives of state-sanctioned violence. As Bond observed: 'Clearly the stoning to death of a baby in a London park is a typical English understatement. Compared to the "strategic" bombing of German towns it is a negligible atrocity, compared to the cultural and emotional deprivation of most of our children its consequences are insignificant' (Bond, 1977, pp. 310–11).

Another significant issue that the depiction of violence in the play raised for some contemporary reviewers was what one might term the 'politics of representation'. The prevailing style of many of the other writers of the 'New Wave' was dramatic naturalism complemented with the relative social realism of Wesker in plays such as *Roots* and *The Kitchen* (1959). Bond's *Saved*, with its urban location and heightened, 'realist' working-class idiom, was therefore presumed to be firmly located within social realism. However, Bond's dramatic style in these formative plays was already exploring issues of dramatic form and language. These were the seeds that would grow into its own distinctive, autonomous identity. Simultaneously Bond was laying the foundations for a powerful new form of political drama.

In the same year that *Saved* was first produced, Bond was a shortlisted finalist for the prestigious award of Most Promising Playwright of 1965. The play opened at the Royal Court Theatre on 3 November 1965. Bond had submitted *Saved* to the theatre on 18 September 1964, but the Lord Chamberlain would not grant a licence for the play to be produced without severe and unacceptable cuts to Bond's script. Gaskill, the play's director, had therefore made a decision to present the play in an implicitly private production. This was essentially for an audience from those ten thousand affiliated members of the English Stage Society. The production was thus a club production, which could be presented outside the jurisdiction of the censor, whose authority existed only over public performances. On 13 December 1965 police officers acting under the authority of the Lord Chamberlain's Office visited the theatre to see a performance of *Saved*. They were not asked to show their membership cards. Therefore, on a technicality (they were in fact members), their presence effectively undermined the 'private' status of the performance. In January 1966 the Royal Court Theatre was charged (under the 1843 Theatres Act) with presenting an unlicensed play. On 14 February 1966 court proceedings opened, while on 17 February theatre censorship was debated in the House of Lords. On 1 April the Royal Court Theatre was found guilty, although the defendants were given a conditional discharge. *Saved* was the last play prosecuted under the censorship laws.

Meanwhile, Bond's next play, *Early Morning* (1968), commissioned by Gaskill, was banned in its entirety by the Lord Chamberlain. Following the same strategy that had ultimately failed with *Saved*, Gaskill decided once more to stage 'private' performances for members of the English Stage Society. This planned production only served to heighten the controversy. The situation reached a public crisis point when the Arts Council threatened to withdraw its funding to the Royal Court Theatre for that specific play if presentation went ahead. Gaskill produced a Sunday evening private performance on 31 March 1968. Police subsequently visited the theatre, though no charges were filed. *Early Morning* proved to be the last play ever to be actually prevented from production by the Lord Chamberlain, although Bond's next play, *Narrow Road to the Deep North* (1968), premiered at The Belgrade Theatre, Coventry in defiance of cuts demanded by the censor. Ultimately, the battle was won as legislation was passed in Parliament on 26 September 1968 to abolish censorship.

In this same year, 1968, Bond continued to receive further recognition, even as the critics remained divided over his work. In May he received the George Devine Award for both *Saved* and *Early Morning* and won the John Whiting Award for *Narrow Road to the Deep North*. Meanwhile, in April 1968, the Conservative MP Enoch Powell gave his infamous 'Rivers of Blood' speech in which he predicted that without the repatriation of many non-white Commonwealth immigrants, interracial violence would erupt across Britain's towns and cities. The Royal Court Theatre organised an agit-prop event against Powell's speech and the racial unrest and violent prejudice that it unleashed. For this event Bond contributed *The Enoch Show* (1969), which on its first performance was disrupted by members of the English neo-Nazi party, the National Front. This right-wing group was the forerunner of the contemporary British National Party (BNP).

In 1969, following the abolition of censorship in the previous autumn, Gaskill brought together a short season of Bond plays (*Saved* and *Early Morning*), each to be given its first unrestricted public performance, along with the London premiere at the Royal Court Theatre of *Narrow Road to the Deep North*. The first public production of *Saved* opened on 19 February 1969 with a new cast featuring Kenneth

Cranham as protagonist Len. It was tellingly reviewed by Martin Esslin for *Plays and Players* (June 1968) as follows:

> Nothing could have shown up the idiocy of British stage censor-ship in its declining phase than the reaction of the public – and even critics! – to the revival of *Saved* at the Royal Court [...] What a brilliant play *Saved* is, and how well it has stood the test of time! [...] *Saved* is a deeply moral play: the scene of the stoning of the baby, which led to the first outcry about it, is one of the key points of its moral structure. (Esslin, 1968, p. 26)

Early Morning represents a change in location, scale and focus from Bond's first two plays, while remaining a play that, as Bond asserted, 'is essentially about working-class life' (Bond qtd in Roberts, 1985, p. 19). It is a savage comedy in which some of the principal historical charac-ters from the late-Victorian political era are relocated in an effectively postmodern domain: a microcosm of the violence and power dynam-ics within British imperialism. This dramatic landscape features not only a lesbian relationship between Victoria and Nightingale but also cannibalistic murders erupting out of the queues waiting to enter an urban London cinema. Further provocation lurked in a sub-narrative in which Benjamin Disraeli and the Prince Consort, Albert, plot to overthrow the monarchy and assassinate Victoria. Bond's savage criti-cism of the brutal self-interest and callous pragmatism of the ruling classes anticipates the murdering British missionary regime of his *Narrow Road to the Deep North*. Equally, although in a more developed generic form, it pre-empts the nightmarish fusion of Stalinism and Auschwitz in the geo-ideological landscape of *Lear* (1971).

Bond's next play, *The Sea*, was first produced at the Royal Court Theatre on 22 May 1973, directed by Gaskill. There is a strong bio-graphical resonance to this play for the dramatist, as Bond was inspired by profound images from his childhood experiences as an evacuee in East Anglia. Bond recalled these memories in an interview in the *Radio Times* (4–10 March 1978):

> The images I had when I wrote *The Sea* go back to my childhood, the war. I was evacuated. Like now, the war was a time of great horror and fear. As if all the horrors in the movies were really coming to life, happening. One afternoon, I remember so clearly

being taken to a photographer's shop. By the coast [...] the studio was upstairs [...] Suddenly I was up there at a giant's height, looking out. And I realised how vast the sea was. And suddenly all the dreadful things about war became very small. The same afternoon I was told the story of somebody walking along the beach, finding the body of someone who had been torpedoed. Washed up [...] It was one of those things when suddenly the world starts asking you questions. (Bond qtd in Roberts, 1985, p. 29)

The Sea is set in an Edwardian east-coast town. It is a microcosm of a world in which the pathological insanity of the character Hatch, a small-town shopkeeper, is exposed as a form of petit bourgeois, xenophobic paranoia. Hatch leads a group of local men in a ludicrous and furtive search for aliens who are intent on taking over the planet by inhabiting human bodies. A drowned young man is tragically washed up on the shore. He becomes for Hatch another chilling example of the endless lengths to which the aliens will go in order to infiltrate decent, conventional human society.

Hatch's rampant paranoia exists alongside, and in diametrical opposition to, the small-town social hierarchy presided over by Mrs Rafi, a marvellous comic character. Rafi is directing her socially conformist female acolytes in a classical drama, with the sanctimonious rationale of raising funds for the local coast guard. The production is being rehearsed in the grande dame's drawing room. Bond wittily uses this play-within-the-play as a means of exposing the tensions, jealousies and neuroses underlying the social status of the female characters. They are ably supported by a classic comic vicar. This scene foregrounds the essentially enacted roles and power strategies of provincial bourgeois life. Hatch's pathological world-view is, in fact, a perfectly logical extension and consequence of the manipulated social charade that poses as polite, decent society. The soundings of the military batteries throughout the play – invisible but present and incessantly intruding – remind the audience of pre-1914 Britain and Europe beyond the narrow confines of the coastal community.

Within this metaphor of the insanity and ideological chaos of late-empire Britain, Bond employs characters who offer some sense of relative calm, sanity and provisional hope for escape and change. The character of Evens is an older man who lives in self-chosen isolation on the beach at the farthest edge of this society. He is able to offer a rational perspective on the underlying causes of the social pathology of the community. He is arguably a fusion of Prospero and Bond. It is an act of conscious irony, as the playwright's Cambridgeshire home in the village of Great Wilbraham is, in Bond's words, 'on the edge of Wilbraham, and I'm known here as "the last man in the village"' (Bond qtd in Hay and Roberts, 1980, p. 8).

In November 1974 Bond contributed to 'Poets for the People' at the Mermaid Theatre in London, an event that raised funds for the Defence Aid Fund of Southern Africa. In 1975 Bond's play *The Fool: Scenes of Bread and Love* opened, another play that takes a writer from a specific historical context and uses him as a means of exploring wider issues. In the case of *The Fool* the writer is the poet John Clare, who lived and worked in rural Northamptonshire in the English Midlands. In a letter to Tony Coult, on 28 July 1977, Bond observed:

> We mustn't only write problem plays, we must write answer plays – at least plays which make answers clearer and more practical ... The answers aren't always light, easy, or even straightforward, but the purpose – a socialist society – is clear. (Qtd in Roberts, 1985, p. 68)

This play is discussed in detail in Chapter 1.

These sentiments throw interesting light upon the plays of what Bond has called his Second Series: *The Fool*; *The Bundle, or, New Narrow Road to the Deep North* (performed and published in 1978); *The Woman: Scenes of War and Freedom* (performed in 1978, published in 1979); *The Worlds* (performed in 1979, published in 1980); and *Restoration* (performed and published in 1981). In their different ways, these plays all seek to propose answers, no matter how provisional and problematic, to the crucial political and social issues facing us and our society in the late twentieth century. *The Bundle* is a reworking of *Narrow Road to the Deep North*, offering an extension of its allegorical structure. As Bond explained in *The Guardian* on 13 January 1978: 'The people in *The Bundle* all live by a river. Directly or indirectly they all live from it. From time to time it floods and destroys them. If, as the play invites, you substitute factories and offices – all industrialism – for the river, then my purpose is plain' (Bond qtd in Roberts, 1985, p. 43).

Bond directed *The Woman* in the Olivier Theatre at the National Theatre in London. This play is set at the time of the Trojan War. Its use of Greek mythology allowed the playwright to further universalise his expression of the horrors of war and superstition. It was the first full-length modern play presented on the main stage of the National Theatre.

The Worlds was given its first production at Newcastle Playhouse on 8 March 1979 and subsequently performed by the Activists' Youth Theatre Club on 21 November 1979 at the Royal Court Theatre Upstairs. Both productions were directed by Bond. Its professional premiere was at the New Half Moon Theatre, London, on 16 June 1981. It broke into newly developed territory. As Bond made clear: 'I'm trying to move towards a theatre in which very often the character is not relating the voice to himself but is relating his voice to the "pictoriality," the picture of the whole stage' (Bond qtd in Roberts, 1985, p. 45). This development in dramatic strategy and focus enabled Bond's central characters to speak with an even more vigorous and direct manner. However, they are not reduced to being mouthpieces. Instead they challenge the assumptions and the prejudices of the ruling classes.

In *The Worlds*, Trench is a managing director of a company whose motivating force is money and its acquisition with a veneer of high-cultural sensibility. Given the continuing crisis in global capitalism and the banking system at the time of writing (2013), Bond's 1981 play proves unerringly prescient of the political and economic conditions some 30 years later. It also offers an essential correlative to the debate between the Tory–Liberal Democrat Coalition government and the Labour Opposition as to the effectiveness of an Inquiry into the causes of the crisis. Bond's play reveals a systemic corruption and hypocrisy within capitalism that could not be amended or resuscitated by pseudo-democratic inquiries of either politicians or the judiciary.

Following the usurpation of his power in a board coup, armed revolutionary political activists aim to kidnap Hibbard, Trench's successor, in order to force the company to meet the wage demands of the workers, whose livelihood is diminishing while the directors continue to increase profits. However, instead of kidnapping Hibbard, they succeed only in abducting his chauffeur.

This scenario provides an opportunity for a rigorous examination of the ways in which human life may be reduced to a commodity within capitalism. Far from being willing to pay the ransom for the chauffeur, Hibbard and his capitalist, bourgeois-gangster associates cynically calculate that the victim has cost more than the ransom fee. Accordingly the victim is in 'debt' to them.

The character that is most articulately resistant to Trench and his self-serving cronies is Terry, a trade union political activist. This choice of character was particularly significant at the time that the play premiered. In this period Thatcher's government had set about passing new legislation that seriously weakened the function of trade unions as representatives and protectors of workers' interests. Terry has several powerful speeches marked by a strong sense of passionate opposition to this corrupt, self-interested status quo. The revolutionary activist Anna also articulates the significance of the title of the play while embodying a political perspective that is central to Bond's own world-view:

ANNA Listen. There are two worlds. Most people think they live in one but they live in two. First there's the daily world in which we live. The world of appearance. There's law and order, right and wrong, good manners. How else could we live and work together? But there's also the *real* world. The world of power, machines, buying, selling, working. That world depends on capital: money! Money can do anything. It gives you the power of giants. The real world obeys the law of money. And there's a paradox about this law: whoever owns money is owned by it [...] Our lives, our minds, what we are, the way we see the world, are not shaped by human law but by the law of money. (*W*, p. 75)

The major plays from this decade thus deal with perennial issues in Bond's work whilst also demonstrating the continuing evolution of ideology and form in the process.

Other plays by Bond in the 1980s included *Summer* (1982), which Bond directed and in which he returned, as in *The Sea*, to Shakespeare's *The Tempest* as a source. *Derek* (1982) is an ideological fable about the political manipulation of a young man's identity and genius. *The Cat* was a relatively rare, collaborative outing into radical music-theatre (performed in English as *The English Cat* in 1983, with music by Hans Werner Henze). As in *Restoration* the genre of music-theatre is used for the exploration of political concerns. All of the characters have animal personae. *Red Black and Ignorant* is a short play that was originally written between December 1983 and January 1984. Its first London production was at the Barbican Theatre, London, in January 1984, directed and designed by Nick Hamm. The following May, a play with the working title 'The Birmingham Play' became *The Tin Can People*. With the addition of *Great Peace* (performed in 1985), these plays were published in 1985 as a new trilogy, *The War Plays*. The war in question is the terrifying possibility, even likelihood, of nuclear holocaust.

In an interview with *The Guardian* on 16 January 1984, Bond spoke of the circumstances surrounding his writing of *Red Black and Ignorant* and of his key concerns expressed in that play:

> When I was asked to write for 'Thoughtcrimes' at the Barbican, I decided to write about nuclear war. A society which does not 'know itself' does not act rationally. If the processes by which the state organises society's various strata and activities are corruptions of the truth, then these corruptions will affect all its decisions ... I created a character that in fact never lives: he is burned in the womb in a nuclear war. His 'ghost' angrily attacks those people who to preserve freedom condemn him and millions of others to the perpetual imprisonment of death. He argues that a society that invests and labours to make that possible, and gambles on having to do it, ought not to be called civilization. (Bond qtd in Roberts, 1985, pp. 52–3)

The whole of *The War Plays* lasts seven hours. Bond was originally going to co-direct the trilogy for the Royal Shakespeare Company at the Barbican in 1985. He left the project in frustration at the standard of the work, however, and described the ensuing Royal Shakespeare Company production as disastrous. He has frequently said that it is one reason why he turned his back on British theatre at that time. That decision, whatever other complex factors might have played their part in it being reached, was to effectively place him in a form of exile from the major British stages. In his insightful article, Saunders discusses this significant and ongoing dimension to the production of Bond's work in Britain:

> A shibboleth has grown up around the work of Edward Bond. The tag 'controversial dramatist' has continued to dog the man

and his work [...] Since the reception of The War Plays (1985) by
the Royal Shakespeare Company at the National Theatre Bond
has largely withdrawn his work from mainstream British theatre.
(Saunders, 2004, p. 256)

Saunders proceeds later in his article to quote from personal correspondence between himself and Bond in relation to this critical
state of affairs:

I found that if I were bound to this country I could no longer do
the work I wanted to do. Theatre here has become restricted. Its
methods are increasingly derived from film and television and
Broadway [...] I talk of exile not as a romantic or angry gesture –
it is merely the logic of my situation. (Bond qtd in Saunders,
2004, p. 265)

The War Plays were later produced in Paris at the Odéon-Théâtre de
l'Europe in 1995, and there have been many productions in Europe
of the whole or parts of the trilogy.

Continuing through the mid and late 1980s, Bond wrote other significant plays, such as *Jackets* (first performed in 1989, published in
1990), in which a woman has two sons, one a soldier and the other
a political revolutionary (terrorist). This short play examines the
interweaving of public and personal narratives within a dramatic site
of urban violence and political unrest. The decade came to a close
with the production of *September* (first performed in 1989, published
in 1990) at Canterbury Cathedral, a seemingly unlikely setting for
a Bond play. Much of his subsequent work has been written specifically for performance by community and young people's groups or
for the Théâtre national de la Colline in Paris, because in Britain,
at least, Bond has become disillusioned with the general theatrical
climate. However, he has continued to be produced extensively in
mainland Europe, with the premiere of *In the Company of Men* (published in 1990, first performed in 1992) and *Coffee*, performed in
2000 at the Théâtre national de la Colline. In France he is the second
most-produced writer, after Molière.

Bond's desire to communicate to young audiences has been synonymous with his working relationship with the Birmingham-based
Theatre in Education company, Big Brum, led for the last decade

by Chris Cooper. The edited transcript of my interview with Chris Cooper constitutes Interview 2 of this study. Bond's plays for young audiences include *Eleven Vests*, first presented by Big Brum Theatre on 7 October 1997 prior to a regional tour of the play. The two parts of this work explore the events surrounding a character known only as the Student. The Student is a teenager who, in the opening part of the play, has been marginalised and subsequently expelled for the seemingly random destruction of other pupils' property. He remains quiet throughout a long interrogation from his Head Teacher, who tries various strategies of inducement and judgemental criticism to try to understand the teenager's actions. Ultimately, the events lead to the Student murdering the Head Teacher with a knife. This dramatic enactment was a powerfully disturbing and controversial echo of an incident that shocked British society in 1995: the knifing to death of a well-respected head teacher, Philip Lawrence, while seeking to intervene in a fight at his school gates. Bond comments: 'I'm sure Philip Lawrence was as innocent as his killer. But in one shape or another, violence always returns to unleash its wrath on the ignorance that creates it. And we are an ignorant society' (Bond, 1997b, p. 35).

In the second half of the play, based again on an actual incident (this time from World War II), the audience sees the Student on active service in the army at war. He murders two defenceless prisoners of war. The street violence enacted at the school gates mirrors the state-sanctioned violence of war and invites the play's young audiences to question both. The themes are the causes and function of violence and the social, cultural and political site in which that violence is enacted. Bond recalled the impact that national military service had on him:

> I didn't like what I saw and I wanted to write about it. There was an atmosphere of violence and coercion. It was a very brutal society. (Bond, 1997b, pp. 96–7)

Tuesday, which was a BBC Schools television drama (and marked Bond's debut as a television director), and other plays such as *At the Inland Sea* (commissioned and first performed by Big Brum in 1995) were written in the context of major changes and debate surrounding compulsory education at this time. This political debate and subsequent policy changes continue. The work of Big Brum and the plays which were commissioned by them from Bond have played a significant role in this ongoing struggle between reactionary and progressive models of education.

Through the late 1990s and into the early years of the twenty-first century, Bond's plays continued to attract interest and sometimes scandal with productions in France and Germany.

Bond's remorseless questioning of human existence and human society has been pursued through a new language of political drama that centres upon the human and our human responsibility to create 'humanness'. It is arguably the case that Bond believes that political drama, to the extent that this term has any sustained contemporary currency, needs to be radically reoccupied and rediscovered. It is my belief that this is a major and central project within both Bond's mid-to-late working life and his plays. Its investigation and interrogation is the central spine of this study. Bond's theoretical writings on the relationship between drama and society in the middle and later plays reflect a complex ontological model and site of drama in relation to human existence. This evolving critical perspective necessitates an ongoing critique of postmodern capitalism. However, the issues surrounding his 'exile' as discussed by Saunders have meant that Bond had remained largely unperformed on the main theatre stages of his native country since the early 1990s. It was not until Jonathan Kent's critically acclaimed revival of *Lear* at the Sheffield Crucible Theatre, followed by Rupert Goold's revival of *Restoration* with his Headlong Theatre, that Bond's plays began to enjoy a new-found visibility. Later still, Kent's West End, Haymarket Theatre production of *The Sea* consolidated that recuperated reputation and a growing critical realisation and reappreciation of Bond's plays. Nevertheless, Bond continues to refuse permission for his plays to be staged by the Royal Shakespeare Company, the Royal Court Theatre and the National Theatre, in spite of their requests to do so. Saunders again offers a necessary perspective from Bond:

> I'm told that I've boxed myself into a corner because I believe only I know how to stage [my plays]. This just isn't true. I don't know how to stage them – I have to find out with actors, and I learn a lot from many productions of my plays by foreign directors [...] I need a community of people who want to create a new theatre – to

begin again from where Euripides stopped. Here [the UK], Euripides is probably the name of a soft drink. (Saunders, 2004, p. 265)

This omission reflects the profound changes in the political and cultural climate in Britain within Bond's working life and also Bond's concern that his plays should be properly understood in the process of their rehearsal and production. Bond says that the most important thing about his career is the necessity he has found of concentrating his work on the European mainland. He frequently comments that he finds it ironic that a British dramatist must go abroad to save British theatre from what he sees as its present tragedy. Bond continues to produce new work and was involved on a film project based on *In the Company of Men*, adapted by director Arnaud Desplechin, Emmanuel Bourdieu and Nicolas Saada, titled *En jouant 'Dans la compagnie des hommes'*. It premiered at the Cannes Film Festival in May 2003. *Have I None*, a play originally produced at the Big Brum Theatre in 2000, was staged by the Théâtre national de la Colline in 2003–4 and revised in 2005. In 2004 Bond wrote *Born*, the third play of the then Colline triptych, which is dedicated to the director Alain Françon. The triptych evolved further into what eventually became referred to by Bond as 'The Colline Pentad' with the addition of two further plays. *Born* premiered at the Avignon Drama Festival in 2006, which also featured the first stage production of the 2000 radio play *Chair* and a revival of the Colline production of *Have I None*. In the first decade of the twenty-first century and continuing with no signs of diminishing energy or momentum into the second decade, there has been a significant re-emergence of Bond's plays upon major British stages as previously identified. Since then, along with his continuing writing for Big Brum with newly commissioned plays such as *Tune* (2007), there have also been critically well-received productions by Rupert Goold's Headlong Theatre of Bond's 1980s *Restoration* (2005) and *Bingo* (2010) at the Chichester Festival Theatre starring Patrick Stewart as Shakespeare. This production was then revived at the Young Vic Theatre in March 2012.

In the autumn of 2010 there was the landmark event of a short season of six of Bond's plays at the newly opened Cock Tavern Theatre in Kilburn which included the world premiere of a new play commissioned for the season called *There Will Be More*.

In November 2011 there was a critically acclaimed revival of *Saved* directed by Sean Holmes at the Lyric Theatre, Hammersmith, London. This production was the prelude to a further short season of later plays at the Lyric, namely *Have I None*, *The Under Room* and *Chair* in April and May 2012. Also throughout 2012 there was an ongoing 'Bond@50' season of events including the performance and rehearsed readings of some of his plays written for Big Brum. There was also a major two-day conference and festival at Warwick University in November 2012 organised by Professor Tony Howard and Chris Cooper.

Following on from Methuen's publication of his major theoretical study on drama and society in 2000 (*The Hidden Plot: Notes on Theatre and the State*), L'Arche, Bond's French publisher, released the French translation in 2003.

Bond frequently holds actors' workshops in Belgium and France under the title 'Acting the Invisible Object'. From actors' exercises developed in such a workshop in Vincennes in 2003, Bond created the play *The Short Electra*, which was among the plays published by Methuen in 2005. These workshops are part of a radical new form of theatre, the fullest description of which can be found in David Davis' edited collection of essays *Edward Bond and the Dramatic Child: Edward Bond's Plays for Young People*. This volume also examines Bond's radical ideas on the nature of reason and imagination, which he considers as hitherto misunderstood. He is in the process of creating 'a rational tragedy' which is characterised and explored in his very latest plays such as *There Will Be More*, which is effectively the first part of his ongoing *Dea* project.

Two volumes of selections from Bond's notebooks were published in 2000 and 2001, edited by Ian Stuart. In one entry, dated 16 April 1980, he wrote:

> I find that my work is more than I had thought. I began writing simply as a criticism of certain things I saw around me and in praise of certain other things. I wanted to understand and so I had to analyse. I didn't at that time understand the implications this would have on my theatrical technique. [An actor] must understand the whole play. What he has to act are the situations. He shows us, not a character acting, but a character being formed [...] in interaction with the world. (Bond, 2001, p. 8)

For Bond there is an enduring, complex interaction between human beings and their world. Intrinsic to this is a seemingly irreconcilable tragic paradox ensuing from that dialectic. It is a defining presence in all of his plays and non-dramatic writings. Over the past 50 years and now into the sixth decade of a remarkably enduring and productive working life, the concepts of humanness, 'radical innocence' and the human imagination as the ontological dramatic site have fought and struggled their way into being.

As I shall argue further in this study, this provocative and evocative dialectical model has been characterised by an increasing awareness of philosophical and ethical complexity.

The tragic, monochrome X-ray after-image of the darkly iconic dead baby hovers above *Saved* in the 1960s through to *The Woman* in the 1970s and into the 1980s through *Red Black and Ignorant*. This haunting image reappeared in *At the Inland Sea* in the 1990s and through into one of his most recent plays *There Will Be More* (2010). It is also, I would argue, a premonition and dark antecedent of the dummy found in the 'later plays' such as *The Children* (2000) and *The Under Room* (2006). Throughout its various incarnations there resonates a silent scream for political, social and ethical justice embodied in that sepulchral leitmotif.

In Chapters 1 and 2 I will explore and discuss the evidence of a renewed dramatic vision and methodology of political drama. Nevertheless I also argue that this re-energised genre is traceable back to the origins of Bond's plays and thinking in his earliest produced work. This sense of an emerging, post-Brechtian, heightened, modernist model of radical drama is especially crucial and pertinent in these traumatic times when Bond asserts that we must learn to 'sing in the ruins' of a human history, witnessing its suicidal catastrophe. As Spencer (1992) observes:

> If strictly realistic and naturalistic modes of address seem outmoded, their conventions too visible, so too do the current modernist experiments that have fuelled the aesthetics of late consumer capitalism. That Bond's work attempts to negotiate this difficult historical moment is hard to deny: the issues are imprinted in the content of the plays, the formal strategies and techniques through which they are mediated, Bond's own critical writing and direction of development, and the kind of success he

has been accorded so far. Whether Bond's plays will provide a productive model, and a way out of the impasse, for a younger generation of politically committed artists, or whether they will remain no more than an illustration of the historical contradictions they embody, is important work for future audiences to decide. (p. 246)

What song might one sing and what words and what tune might one find are questions central not only to the understanding and production of Edward Bond's writing. They are maybe also the inescapable questions crucial to our understanding and transformation of our contemporary society and world.

Edward Bond is an advocate of the imperative necessity of a theatre whose central function is, as he said in a 2000 *Guardian* interview, 'to recreate what it means to be human, to redefine our relationship with the world'. The dramatist's problem, he added, is 'how do you speak sanity to the insane?' (Logan, 2000). At the time of writing (2013) it is my belief that Bond, among other concerns, is seeking to articulate a potentially major new development and stage in his theoretical thinking and playwriting.

In this Introduction I have described a trajectory across the entirety of Bond's creative output. The intention was to offer an 'aerial map' of some of the key cairns or way-marks on Bond's journey as a playwright. It also helps map the topography of Bond's development as a theoretician of the relationship between drama and society.

I now identify the key defining concepts in the evolution of his theoretical position. This anticipates the substantial detailed discussion of Bond's plays in Chapters 1 and 2. The first chapter, 'Your Morality is Violence', focuses upon the extent to which Bond revisited the past from a broadly Marxist perspective in four major works: *Lear* (1971), *Bingo* (1974), *The Fool* (1975) and *Restoration* (1981). In addition to traversing an important decade in Bond's writing these plays also correspond to what Bond refers to elsewhere as his 'first' to early 'middle' periods. It is my belief that the important plays from this decade present amongst the most significant achievements prior to the best achievements of more recent work.

Chapter 2, 'Learning to Sing in the Ruins', therefore examines a selection of these 'later plays', starting with *The Crime of the Twenty-First Century* (1999). These have continued through to his most recent work, at the time of writing, such as *Dea* (in progress), *The Broken Bowl* (2012) and *The Edge* (2012).

In the Conclusion, 'Was Anything Done?', I offer a concluding reflection surveying the central issues of this study, articulating my own current re-evaluation of the significance of Bond's work.

An integral component of my research are two interviews. The first is an interview with Sean Holmes, Artistic Director of the Lyric Theatre, Hammersmith, London. Holmes had proposed the season of Bond plays at the Lyric and directed *Saved* in autumn 2011 as well as *Have I None* from 'The Chair Plays' – three later Bond plays produced in spring 2012. The second interview, mentioned earlier, is with Chris Cooper, the Artistic Director of Big Brum Theatre in Education company in Birmingham. Bond has been commissioned on a regular basis to write plays for their tours of schools in Birmingham and the region since 1995. I met and talked with Chris Cooper in Birmingham in June 2012. This interview took place immediately prior to a rehearsed reading revival in Birmingham of *At the Inland Sea* with members of the original cast: Bobby Colvill, Mandy Finney and Terina Talbot. Cooper was also in the middle of a tour of Bond's play *The Broken Bowl*, which he was re-rehearsing at that point. These conversational interviews are important for two reasons.

Firstly, they reinforce one of my central approaches in this study. That is an approach which views and discusses Bond's plays *as* plays intended ultimately for performance. My in-depth engagement with and analysis of key themes and dramatic devices in Bond's plays is in direct interface with the material circumstances of their realisation. Secondly, in direct relationship to this, the interviews with Holmes and Cooper provide a unique opportunity for the plays to be discussed practically from the perspective of their rehearsal and production. At the time of the interview with Holmes I was deeply immersed in a production of Bond's *The Children* I was rehearsing with undergraduate students at the University of Winchester. This facilitated some rich insights into the challenges facing the realisation of Bond's plays in practice.

We've come to the river: navigating Bond's critical theory

At the risk of reductive simplification, the key concepts informing Bond's strategies as a dramatist can be identified in a broadly chronological framework. They start with Bond's 'Rational Theatre' (incorporating his concept of 'aggro-effects'). This emerged initially in the first phase of his writing career. This was followed by his evolving sense of the centrality of 'theatre events', which represented a deepening and more complex development of his seminal critical model. The next crucial, critical way-mark came with his concept of human imagination as the 'dramatic site' directly and integrally related to his concept of 'radical innocence'. These terms, I believe, continue to exercise a profound influence upon his thinking and writing. Out of that process have emerged associated and current concepts such as the 'Internal Transcendent', the 'Human Imperative' and the 'Third Crisis'. I want to stress that these staging-posts are offered in this context as preliminary 'critical shorthand'. I should also add that the evolution of Bond's thinking is not narrowly linear but rather organic and interwoven. The potent stage image of the catatonic young man surrounded by the detritus of tinned foods, themselves a metaphor of an emerging consumer culture, is a powerful example of such a seminal 'theatre event'. I also believe that later emerging concepts such as 'radical innocence' and the 'Internal Transcendent' signalled a particular and very significant sea change in Bond's 'later plays'. There is an irresistible, organic relationship between those earlier critical currents and their subsequent later sea-swell. This inherent interconnectedness is of crucial importance in understanding and analysing Bond's work and achievements. Bond's key critical concepts are axiomatic in defining the evolution of an emerging hybrid methodology of radical, political drama. I discuss this in detail in Chapter 2, and identify and explain how these 'later plays' are comprised of two major series. The first series is what Bond initially called 'The Colline Pentad', after the theatre for which they were originally written, to be staged by its Artistic Director Alain Françon. According to Bond (his notes in *Plays: 8* and *Plays: 9*), only the first three plays were staged at the Théâtre national de la Colline – Françon left La Colline and staged the two remaining plays elsewhere in Paris. It therefore seemed appropriate to Bond to rename the series 'The Paris Pentad'. The plays in this series are *Coffee*, *The Crime of the Twenty-First Century*, *Born*, *People* and *Innocence*. My discussion of this series focuses upon *The Crime of the Twenty-First Century* and *Innocence*.

The second series Bond refers to as 'The Birmingham Plays'. This generic term refers to all of Bond's plays written for Big Brum from 1995 through to the present. I focus my discussion of 'The Birmingham Plays' on *Chair*, *Have I None*, *The Under Room* and *Tune*. Some of the plays originally commissioned by Big Brum were then also produced in Paris, such as *Have I None*.

'The dance of things in themselves'

In the remainder of this Introduction I want to offer some further perspectives on the major themes and concerns identified in Bond's work. Inevitably over such a long and productive working life, Bond's plays and his thinking can be seen to have changed at times in emphasis and focus. Nevertheless, it is one of the major aims of this study to suggest an unbroken spine of dramaturgy and methodology throughout his working life.

Bond reflected in a notebook entry, dated as early as 21 February 1960, and entitled 'Note on Dramatic Form':

> We need a new dramatic form not simply because we want a bright new package in which to sell what we have to say; or because we want to start a new fashion that will catch the public's eye. We need a new form because the old form falsifies experience. The form of the Ibsenite well-made play, derived from the Greeks via the Renaissance, isn't related to the subject of the play, in the way that a picture-frame is usually related to a picture. (Bond, 2000c, p. 49)

Against this wider background of opposing and criticising a drama that 'falsifies experience', Bond also challenged and disassociated his plays and thinking from Brecht. Bond became increasingly critical about what in wider political and cultural debate had become the 'given' neo-orthodoxies of Brechtian theatre. That influential model had by the onset of Bond's work as a dramatist become a shibboleth of Left-oriented political theatre. The Brechtian model had played a leading role in the definition of the genre of 'political theatre' from the early and mid decades of the twentieth century. Its impact had been principally on the continent and in German theatre in particular. From 1956 onwards, when the Berliner Ensemble first visited

Britain and whom Bond saw at the Royal Court, it informed debate within the liberal-left theatre and its practitioners:

> Perhaps the most important single event at this period was the visit of Brecht's Berliner Ensemble to London in July and August 1956, with productions of *Mother Courage, Trumpets and Drums* and *The Caucasian Chalk Circle*. Bond was [...] massively impressed with the work of the Berliner [...] that experience gelled with his responses to Wolfitt's [*sic*] *Macbeth*, for he saw aspects of the Berliner style as resembling the style of the earlier actor-manager companies. (Hay and Roberts, 1980, p. 16)

Bond's initial interest in Brecht's work in this period was, however, to be increasingly revisited, revised and ultimately upturned. The broader influence of Brecht across European theatre up until that time might be viewed as a form of methodological 'frame'. Through this it had became possible in both the post-World War I and later post-1945 periods to formulate some of the fundamental questions about the relationship between politics and theatre. Bond's observation that the naturalist/realist genre epitomised by Ibsen 'falsifies experience', and his subsequent critiquing of Brecht, are crucial to an understanding of Bond's journey. Whereas Bond, in *The Pope's Wedding*, arguably intends a dramatic disjuncture through the murder and Scopey's subsequent action, it is not as some earlier critics averred a seminal example of Bond employing Brechtian alienation effects. My view is that the device might owe as much to Bond's exposure to Ionesco just prior to that period. The existential and ontological dramatic site on which Scopey's murdering of Alen takes place and his subsequent actual and metaphorical redressing of his own clothes and angst into a transposed alter ego-identity of the dead man, invites the audience onto a deeper level of understanding and discourse. It is arguable that the ideological and dramatic differences between Bond's socialism of that period and Ionesco's nihilism made any further shared exploration effectively impossible.

Bond clearly has a strong sense of participating in a significant historical project in terms of his writing and its contribution to the historical narrative of European theatre. This he pursues with tenacious, unyielding intensity and integrity. For Bond to initiate and articulate a project on this scale without acknowledging the pre-existing legacy of Brecht would be problematic. This is not the case. Acknowledgement is not necessarily synonymous with Bond's unconditional or uncritical acceptance of Brecht's contribution. As Spencer observes in her important, detailed discussion of Bond's pre-1992 plays:

> While Brechtian strategies may prove an appropriate *entry* to an understanding of Bond's plays, they are not enough [...] Without further development of a critical discourse appropriate to Bond's drama, and without closer, more subtle readings of actual plays, scholars run the risk of repeating the mistakes of [...] reproducing the very divisions between politics and aesthetics that so many playwrights since Brecht have tried to move beyond. (Spencer, 1992, p. 11)

It is a core intention of this study to engage in a 'critical discourse appropriate to Bond's drama' based principally upon 'closer, more subtle readings of actual plays'. In so doing it is also my intention to evidence an argument for a recognition and understanding of 'politics and aesthetics' in Bond's work. It represents, I believe, an important and ultimately separate development from Brecht.

As already noted, there is little sustained evidence of any explicit Brechtian dramaturgy in the early, first period of plays such as *The Pope's Wedding* and *Saved*. In *Restoration* (1981), one of the major plays from Bond's middle period, the non-naturalistic use of songs acts to expose ideological contradictions in the play. This understandably evokes for many Brecht's own use of songs to interrogate and comment upon dialectics to disrupt the illusion of narrative hegemony. Nevertheless, in *Restoration*, whilst Bond undoubtedly seeks, 20 years on from his notebook entry, to challenge and avoid the falsification of experience, it is not through alienation effects. What *Restoration* explores centrally, with a fusion of mordant satirical wit and uncompromising political engagement, is a pre-existing historical relationship between capital and the aristocracy based on mutually cynical, powerful self-interest. Bond equally explores ways in which a potentially radicalised working class becomes depoliticised through misplaced, reactionary deference.

Dramatic naturalism at its zenith could evoke a simulacrum of bourgeois social and cultural reality. In Ibsen's finest plays such as

Hedda Gabler it could also expose the volcanic strata of psychological repression and violence unleashed by social and moral hypocrisy. Brecht sought to assert a dialectical counterweight to the shadows of melodramatic emotionalism and destined 'inevitability' which even Ibsen's major works could never quite escape. If dramatic naturalism excelled as a conjuring of the simulacrum of bourgeois socio-cultural reality, Brechtian theatre sought to expose and analyse the socio-cultural and political mechanisms of that apparatus. It wants to know and show *how* and *why* it works, as Spencer elucidates:

> Classic realism may support the dominant ideology by [...] posing problems too limited or too easily resolved to be significant [...] presenting social contradictions in terms of psychological conflicts [...] or representing reality and human nature as ahistorical, eternal, or essentially unchanging. (Spencer, 1992, p. 5)

One of the key differences and disagreements between Bond and Brecht lies in the diagnosis of Brecht's political analysis and the dramatic means which he proposed as remedy. Equally Bond was critical of Brecht agreeing to work under the social, cultural and political conditions of Cold War, Stalinist East Germany.

Earlier in his writing, in the late 1960s and into the 1970s, Bond's essays on his plays and his use of concepts such as 'Rational Theatre' and 'aggro-effects' suggest an adjacency to Brecht in plays like *Narrow Road to the Deep North* (1968). Also in subtitles to plays such as *Bingo: Scenes of Money and Death* (1973) one can see those concepts as residually symptomatic of a particular stage in Bond's development as a dramatist. At certain defining moments in Bond's writing and thinking, his sympathetic identification with a Marxist-based socialism inevitably affected an assumption of proximity between the writers. This is understandable. It is important however to realise that this was not an enduring adjacency.

It appears that Bond grew to be increasingly critical of what he viewed as Brecht's reductive scientific-positivism underlying Epic Theatre. He may have viewed this model as an insufficient means of political analysis and politicised dramatic resolution. I believe that this was acutely reinforced for Bond by the failure of Eastern communism in the Soviet Union: the system had profoundly failed to materialise a Marxist vision of freedom and justice. The fact that

Brecht worked in and was resourced by a repressive regime seriously undermined and compromised Brecht's purportedly revolutionary theatre. Far from facilitating a revolutionary Marxist society characterised by justice and equality, the East German authorities ran a regime which actively silenced opposition. This substantially undermined for some the credibility of Brecht producing avowedly transformative political theatre. It is not surprising therefore that, by the early 1990s, and simultaneous with the inception of his 'Paris Plays' and 'Birmingham Plays', Bond may have come to view Marx's vision as essentially utopian. Most controversially he described Brechtian theatre as 'the theatre of Auschwitz'.

In 'Letter on Brecht', which is a letter from Bond to Rudolf Rach dated 18 March 2000 and published in *The Hidden Plot*, Bond places his provocative assertion within the following context:

> I called the theatre of the A-effect the theatre of Auschwitz. Obviously I do not mean this in a simple sense. In a simple sense it is the opposite of true. The Nazis at Auschwitz would have exterminated Brecht not staged him. Brecht spent his energies and his life trying to make hell-holes such as Auschwitz – or the Gulag – impossible. (Bond, 2000b, p. 171)

In expressing the imperative of nevertheless disassociating himself from Brecht – 'I cannot be if I am to write of our times' – Bond argues that Brecht is now associated with a 'redundant paradigm of knowledge' (Bond, 2000b, p. 173). It is arguable that Bond felt that in the context of working as a beneficiary of the East German regime, Brecht's theatre became corrupt by collusion. Finally, the subtext of this troubling and complex narrative is Bond's strong sense that, in disassociating reason from imagination, the 'alienation effect' was one which was existentially and politically reactionary. If reason is orphaned from imagination and wilfully constrained by the actual and ideological barriers of a wall that Bond's *Lear* built, consciousness is not liberated but rather has all the autonomy and freedom of the ventriloquist's dummy.

What all of these various competing and complex factors contributed to achieve was a deepening conceptual basis by which to understand the nature and function of drama. It also facilitated a means to evaluate its significance politically, culturally and ethically for humans and their society. Out of this decade of new opportunities for Bond in France (especially Paris) and Birmingham, developed his concepts of the 'dramatic site' and 'radical innocence'. Bond's continuing and deepening exploration of drama signifying an onto-logical and existential function had, by *At the Inland Sea* in 1995, signalled an exciting and provocative new model of political drama and theatre.

Against the backdrop of his class background and formative experi-ence of the traumatic dislocations of wartime evacuation and post-war national service, Edward Bond was committed to developing a new, progressive, dramatic form and language. Equally his politici-sation in his early adult life, provoked in part by national service, developed against a backdrop of 1960s radical social and cultural activism. These values necessitated a dramatic form and structure which would inevitably reflect some of the pre-existing and contem-poraneous radical theatre practice:

> The past is the shore – and for dramatists that is Chekhov, Ibsen, Strindberg, Brecht. A modern writer needs those writers and many more – and many painters, musicians and novelists. *But they are not in the maelstrom with you.* There has to be a new beginning. It is new not as a matter of literary fashion. (Bond, 2000b, p. 172)

Crucially Bond was to make an indelible contribution to the still-emerging form and identity of political drama. As Hirst argues:

> Bond has chosen a path very different from [other] political-ly-committed writers [...] His handling of dramatic techniques mir-rors precisely his treatment of social and political structures. Just as he sees it as necessary to understand the history of Britain's social and political institutions in order to change them, so too he has progressively come to realise that as particular dramatic genres are representative of ideals and ideas of their time, it is by [...] adapting them that the responsible playwright can most effectively operate. (Hirst, 1985, p. 7)

I believe that Bond's intention increasingly was and is to facilitate audience *engagement* rather than provoke a Brechtian *disengagement.* In a notebook entry, dated 24 November 1959, and dealing with

Bond's initial background writing and thoughts about *The Pope's Wedding*, he refers to his wrestles with this challenge:

> I have to describe things and events as they are in themselves [...] Obviously I can't alter completely the appearance of things [...] otherwise the audience will not be able to identify [...] Yet, although I must capture 'the dance of things in themselves', things are only present as perceptions in the mind, and so presumably I will be figuring the things onstage as to what they are to the tramp, even though I write them, here, as what they are to themselves. (Bond, 2000c, pp. 42–3)

These thoughts and concerns are the seeds of what would continue to develop through creative endeavour and struggle in the following 50 years of his writing. Most crucially, they reveal his tacit and growing realisation of how drama is a material site of the imagination. It is also the crucible for the radical reimagining of the material, social and political realities of the world. Brecht used the mask in *The Good Person of Szechwan* as a visual alienation device to expose the culturally conditioned dialectics of gender and empowerment. Whereas Shen Te in *The Caucasian Chalk Circle* put on a mask to 'become' her masculinised alter ego Shui Ta, Scopey, in *The Pope's Wedding*, knows that wearing a mask can never be enough except for purposes of deception and disguise. In one important sense the mask reinforces the political and cultural status quo and one's presence within it. Scopey needs to *enter* and *become* the skull *within* and ultimately go beyond the mask. For him, the 'impossible ceremony' that Bond refers to in relation to the play's title evokes Marat's revolutionary call to arms in Peter Weiss' play *Marat/Sade* (1965), 'The important thing is to pull yourself by your own hair, To turn yourself inside out and see the whole world with fresh eyes.'

As Bond observed in an interview with Ulrich Koppen:

> Why are the Greeks so important to us? They took the basic elements of imagination and examined it. All Greek plays deal with basic relationships, have basic stories, in which psychology is related to society in certain ways through authority [...] And it was all the word of God, and could not be changed. God was the storyteller. (Koppen, 1997, p. 103)

Billy in *Chair* seeks to define and control the unstable, threatening reality through his drawings, becoming a *de facto* God 'storyteller', and indeed he tells a long parabolic story to Alice. In *The Pope's Wedding* Scopey mistakenly seeks to exert, with tragic consequences, a psycho-dramatic expression of incontrovertible authority. Even this exertion of a quasi 'papal' infallibility cannot authorise and make real his profoundest emotional and ontological needs.

In *Saved* (1965), revived with such energy and vision by Sean Holmes and with Bond's active engagement in the critically acclaimed 2011 Lyric Theatre production, we have one of the most iconic and defining British plays of the post-war period. The circumstances surrounding the play's first production have been well documented by previous writers and scholars (notably Browne, 1975, and Hay and Roberts, 1980). My intention is not therefore to re-enter that critical area in a narrowly socio-historical sense. As Lacey succinctly observes:

> The critical furore that rapidly enveloped the play was in one sense a focus for a more general anxiety about the limits of the new realism and centred largely on Scene Six, which includes the stoning of a baby on stage. (Lacey, 1995, p. 146)

Whilst Lacey goes on to discuss and locate the play exclusively in terms of social realism, 'There is no doubt that Bond is pursuing a realist project in these plays – to show how things really are' (Lacey, 1995, p. 48), I believe that *Saved* needs to be viewed and interpreted within a more complex, coded generic hybridism. As with any play that acquires an epoch-defining status, there arises not so much the issue of 'guilty by association' but rather 'trapped by interpretation'. With *Saved*, the enduring image of a pram in a South London park became an effectively fetishised cultural icon of sublimated rage with disturbing connotations of lawlessness and social chaos. This materialist stage property, with its correlating semiotic readings of domesticity, vulnerability and innocence, transmuted into a meta-theatrical totemic object of 'shock' and reactionary moral judgement. This has effectively precluded and made problematic other critical readings of the play. Like a pram blocking a path in the park at dusk, there seems to be no way around it. What remains inside that pram has historically compromised the dominant or sole reading of the play's meaning and significance. By gazing into the pram one is corralled into a myopic and calcifying interpretation of *Saved*. The implication in terms of other critical, interpretative readings is a privileging of the micro-materialist location of the park. Accordingly this necessitates the marginalisation of the macro-location of Bond's evolving dramaturgy. Something crucial is missed, if not evaded. In *Saved*, Bond creates effectively fraternal combatants for Scopey. Fred, Mike, Pete and the others are not so much his descendants as his imagined other selves. They share similar social and ultimately political needs. Their actions are also arguably symptomatic of a deeper existential if not ontological disjuncture. Those complex and, in some respects, competing needs are simultaneously located and exploited in a very clear social, cultural and political materiality.

Displaced desire and existential angst interwoven with a political critique of marginalised lives reveal that Bond at this seminal stage is travelling a road where there is no easily visible route ahead. Bond recognised that, albeit with key collaborators at crucial stages, he must name that direction and walk that path alone.

In his most recent philosophical writings on the nature and function of drama within human existence, society and culture, Bond has introduced a new concept of the 'Internal Transcendent'. Bond's concept of the 'Internal Transcendent' resonates with elements of Kant's concepts of the 'categorical imperative' and the 'supra-sensible system'. For Bond, it seems, the categorical driving force of the human mind is the structure of drama in the mind which derives from this imperative – as if the intention of drama (in the mind) were to make active this imperative in instances that define humanness. For Kant by contrast the 'categorical imperative' is the 'fundamental law of pure, practical reason' (Kant qtd in Want and Klimowski, 2011, p. 13). Clearly for Kant the power of the imagination in enhancing reason and knowledge as expressed in the notion of 'suprasensibility' is inextricably linked to his central defining assertion of a 'moral law'. This is a problematic concept and open to reactionary readings and implications. It relates to the human capacity for freedom but also of knowledge and human mutuality. Bond's employment of the 'Internal Transcendent' and its umbilical relationship to 'radical innocence' is crucial I believe in anticipating a major new development in his dramaturgy. It is a fusion of those quasi-Hegelian elements in Marxist thinking regarding the dialectic. Whereas Bond had as recently as his interview with this author in

2006 (Billingham, 2007) resisted the essentialist, Hegelian concept of the 'World Spirit', might it be that in the 'Internal Transcendent' there is a potential correlation of both? The clear difference lies in the foregrounding of materiality in both Marx's and subsequently Bond's thinking. What brings Bond's evolving thinking into an unlikely but potentially exciting union of elements of Kantian and Hegelian metaphysics and Marxist dialectical materialism is Bond's recognition of the dialectical materiality and logic of imagination. The emerging dialectic between Bond's earlier Marxist material-ism and Kantian metaphysical resolution of rational and empir-ical means to knowledge reaches its apotheosis in the 'Internal Transcendent'. It is my view that this concept is not to be viewed or understood as exclusively or essentially metaphysical. Perhaps it would be more helpful to consider the term as broadly equivalent to Raymond Williams' structures of feeling? In this context it is open to discussion and further debate that the term 'Internal Transcendent' might represent the possibility of signalling the specific but equally elusive relationship and dialectics between the individual and their consciousness and the ensuing relationship between the individual consciousness and the objectivity of external reality and society.

Bond unequivocally reaffirms his belief that the concept of the subjective 'self/mind' and the 'objective world/society' are mutually interdependent material realities. In his essay 'The Reason for Theatre' he states:

> The newborn child is on both sides of its skin. There is no outside so it generates its own experiences. Its self is bound into imagi-nation as language is bound into grammar. (Bond, 2000b, p. 114)

One can trace some of the antecedents of this form of thinking as early as his essay 'On Violence' (Bond, 1987). In the specific context of artic-ulating a rationale for his writing and a response to the initial critical reception of *Saved*, he asserted that, 'All imagination is political' (1987, p. 5). This radical deconstruction of the central post-Romantic privileg-ing of the imagination as inherently subjective and esoterically spiritual is further developed in Bond's landmark essay 'The Rational Theatre':

> Literature is a social act; it is the social expression of thought and uses the social medium of language. Yet a creative act comes

through an individual [...] a writer writes what he has experienced and learned (what else can he write about?) but he does not write about himself. What used to be called the soul is really the most public aspect of a human being. (Bond, 1978, p. xi)

In stating so, Bond not only interrogates and exposes the materiality of imagination and writing and dramatic art as cultural production, but also simultaneously and inevitably raises the question of the metaphysics or poetics of cultural materialism. As already discussed, Bond arguably believes that a classical and certainly reductive Marxist reading of human history has been irreversibly compromised. This may reflect his recognition that revolutionary political change has not been realised through a radicalisation of class consciousness within and through a proletarian vanguard. Nevertheless, Bond seems to acknowledge the efficacy of a Marxist analysis of the inherent inequalities and exploitation of the capitalist model of economic organisation. In his earlier critical writings from the 1970s through to the mid 1980s, Bond's recognition of the symbiotic relationship between capitalist economic organisation and cultural production clearly embodied significant elements of a Marxist reading of base and superstructure. Nevertheless, from the emergence of his concept of 'radical innocence' in the mid/late 1990s and the subsequent evolving of the 'Internal Transcendent', the philosophical and dramaturgical site was being consolidated. This was through a dialectical fusion that reflected an interrogation of Marxist materialism and a neo-Kantian ethical ontology of the imagination. From this process a radical new dialectical hybrid was and continues to emerge. It is as paradoxical and provocative as the titles of many of Bond's plays. The dialectical paradox is the gap between a Marx-influenced materialism which rejects any possibility of a Hegelian or Kantian concept of the metaphysical. It also challenges therefore the Kantian noumenal metaphor of transcendence. Bond believes that the materiality of the human imagination simultaneously has its own self-reflexive means of the revolutionising of consciousness through radical innocence and Internal Transcendence. This is located and enacted on the 'dramatic site' of the human imagination. The potential impact that this has on the nature and possibility of political drama is substantive. Whilst propaganda and agit-prop as a genre have never featured in Bond's work outside of earlier consciousness-raising commissions such as the Anti-Apartheid Movement (*Black Mass*, 1970) and the Campaign for Nuclear Disarmament (*Passion*, 1971), the more explicitly political intentions and agendas of plays such as *Narrow Road to the Deep North*, *Jackets* and *The War Plays* exist in counterbalance to a growing and deepening focus upon the ontological and with it the moral, ethical and transcendent.

1
Your Morality is Violence: Politicising the Past

Edward Bond made the following entry dated 2 July 1970 in his notebook: 'In a capitalist society, crime makes an honest man of you' (Bond, 2000c, p. 106). In this chapter I shall explore a series of plays spanning from 1971 to 1981, through which Bond revisited aspects of Britain's social, cultural and political past. It is possible that Bond aimed to investigate and expose the political conflicts and sea change of what was a tumultuous period of social and economic upheaval. This is not, however, to offer a deductive and narrowly singular reading of these complex and important plays. The four plays that constitute the narrative spine of this chapter therefore are, in chronological order, *Lear* (1971), *Bingo: Scenes of Money and Death* (1973), *The Fool: Scenes of Bread and Love* (1975) and *Restoration* (1981).

Some of Bond's most powerful work in the first 20 years of his writing career came in the 1970s, a time of political unrest and activism leading up to the election of Margaret Thatcher's Conservative government in 1979. This was a decade of mass oppositional left-wing political activity. This was particularly so in industrialised northern England and focused upon the major miners' strikes. It was a period which saw the final years of Harold Wilson's Labour administration which had first been elected to power in 1964. In 1970 Wilson called a 'snap' (sudden) election fully expecting to win against a weakened Conservative Party and Shadow Cabinet led by the seemingly unpopular Edward Heath. In fact Heath was elected and Labour would not return to power until 1974 after Heath's economic policies arguably created more social and economic unrest. The new Conservative government pursued a policy of confronting the unions and their political and economic power against the backdrop of an international crisis in oil prices. In 1971 there was a strike of 280,000 British miners. Power stations were targeted with secondary strike action and in 1973 the second strike provoked Edward Heath's Conservative government into declaring a State of Emergency. This resulted in the forced introduction of a three-day working week in order to conserve energy resources.

This was also the decade in British politics when the presence of British troops in Northern Ireland underwent a traumatic transformation. From what had been presented by the government and mainstream media as a 'benign' occupation of British troops to 'protect' a politically and economically vulnerable Catholic community, a tragic transformation occurred. Provoked by a scenario which escalated with appalling rapidity into effectively a state of war following the tragedy of 'Bloody Sunday' in 1972, and through a dark deployment of Orwellian 'double-speak', this violent conflict between the British state and the Irish Catholic people became referred to in public discourse as 'The Troubles'. Bond's engagement with some of the major political events of that era may be seen in shorter plays such as *Black Mass* (1970) and *Passion* (1971). Reflecting Bond's willingness at this time to write a form of agit-prop drama for specific political purposes and contexts, both plays were written for two organizations with clear political aims and strategies. These were respectively the Anti-Apartheid Movement (AAM) and the Campaign for Nuclear Disarmament (CND). In the short provocative piece commissioned by the AAM a small but interesting footnote in modern British theatre history occurred, with Bond himself playing the part of Christ in the opening performance of *Black Mass*. This remains the sole occasion in which Bond appeared in his own work – albeit a non-speaking part.

With *Lear* (1971) Edward Bond produced one of his lifelong, landmark achievements as a dramatist. In this work, Bond's dramatic and political vision challenges, with profound implications, the nature of totalitarian power enforced by state-authorised violence. It also, with equivalent power and resonance, interrogates the central tenets of the genres of classical and neo-classical Renaissance dramatic tragedy. In doing so, in his radical reimagining of Shakespeare's *King Lear*, Bond challenges the concept of a passive, fatalistic catharsis underpinning conventional dramatic tragedy. That is, that human suffering must and will happen and reflects and embodies an inherently fractured, unchangeable human condition. This biological and existential stasis has violence as its gravitational force. In his Preface to *Plays: 2* he wrote:

> Violence shapes and obsesses our society and if we do not stop being violent we have no future. People who do not want writers to write about violence want to stop them writing about us and our time. It would be immoral not to write about violence. (Bond, 1978, p. 3)

As Hirst also identifies:

> *Lear* is a play about revolution. It is also a play about violence. Though the two themes are complementary they are not synonymous, and it may be that the excessive amount of realistic physical violence in this play – far more than in any of Bond's previous dramas [...] considerably alienated reviewers and public alike when the play was first performed. (Hirst, 1985, p. 132)

The question that Hirst's comments raise of a play's capacity to alienate public response through its depiction and use of violence is important. It necessitates examining the relationship between a work of art as a cultural product with its dialectical inscription of its ideological conditions of production. The politically manipulated, mediated representation and reporting of such atrocities as 'Bloody Sunday' effectively seeks to anaesthetise public perception of those events. In the context of the tragic events in Derry it provoked many more years of armed struggle and tragic loss of combatant and civilian lives. It was to be nearly 40 years after the events of 'Bloody Sunday' before a more complete and complex truth could be presented following the Saville Inquiry. Finally published in 2010 after a 12-year period since its formation, the Inquiry's report condemned the actions of the British troops.

The fundamental question of what form of dramaturgy is most effective and appropriate to explore and expose such political violence, and the ethical issues arising from it, seems to have preoccupied Bond over the course of his writing career. It is a question with which I believe he continues to struggle with characteristically unflinching honesty and rigour. In the early and mid seventies when *Lear* and *Bingo* were being written and produced, Bond began to further question the ideological and methodological efficacy of

Brechtian dramaturgy, talking instead in terms of his concept of 'Rational Theatre'.

For Bond at this period the notion of the 'rational' arguably carried a clear connotation of his then Marxist interpretation of society, culture, economy and history:

> An artist cannot create art, cannot demonstrate his objective truth, in the service of reaction or fascism; because art is not merely the discovery of new truth or new aspects of old truth – but also of the human need for the rational [...] Art isn't the discovery of particular truths in the way science is; it also demonstrates the practical working out of the human need for truth. (Bond, 1978, p. xv)

Further on in this Introduction to *Plays: 2*, Bond looks to differentiate and discuss some of the ideological and methodological differences between Brecht's concept of the 'alienation effect' with his own emerging dramaturgy:

> Brecht was against undue empathy; but there is a proper empathy in the love of truth. Drama embodies human experience into its descriptions of history. We are ourselves because we are also history [...] To talk of objectivity in Brecht's sense may well be misleading. Dramatists can't treat their experiments as scientists treat theirs because the experimentation – as much as the struggle and effort outside the theatre – is an event in human life and history. Society is a surgeon operating on himself and art is part of that operation. (Bond, 1978, p. xv)

In the four plays of this period under discussion one sees Bond exploring the political and ethical tensions between the individual and a repressive state. In the case of the character Lear, the oppressor transforms into the oppressed. In *Bingo* and *The Fool*, the focus is upon the compromised writer. With *Restoration*, Bond uses Bob, Rose and Bob's mother as the generic class-based victims of a profoundly reactionary eighteenth-century English governing culture. Significantly, however, as I discuss later in this chapter, it is Rose alone who understands the politics of her class's oppressed condition and seeks to challenge it. There is evidence throughout Bond's dramaturgy of his interrogation of repressive political systems employing violence as a means of sustaining their vested power and self-interest. However, in direct tandem with this rational analysis of political struggle, is a complex, non-sentimental empathy – if not compassion – for those who are the victims of violence. But this is never a simplistic binary in Bond's writing, and in *Lear*, especially, the origins of violence and its oppressive impact are explored across and within the oppressor and the oppressed. This is especially the case in Bond's dramatic treatment of Lear, his two daughters and, finally, Cordelia the revolutionary leader.

Lear (1971)

Reviewing *Lear* for *The Times* on 30 September 1971, Irving Wardle was full of praise for the play and production, reflecting the turnaround in critical reception of Bond's work at this period, following the initial and widely shared denunciation of *Saved*:

> Lear [...] wanders the country in ragged incognito, witnessing Goya-like enormities which befall those who do him small acts of kindness [...] Bond himself has not changed; and we have no other playwright remotely like him. (Qtd in Roberts, 1985, p. 23)

In an interview in the *Performing Arts Journal* in 1976, Bond talked about why he had felt the overwhelming need to revisit Shakespeare's outstanding tragedy on his own terms:

> The reason I took *Lear* is that as a myth it seems central to people's experience. *Lear* is the family tragedy, magnified to the dimensions of political tragedy, state tragedy, and it seems to deal with very fundamental desires and fears that people have. It's a fascinating play [...] and I felt that somehow I wasn't living in the real world until I dealt with that myth on my own terms [...] I think it's the greatest play written, and it's the play I get the most out of. Nevertheless, it doesn't work for me, and in a sense, I have to criticize it. (Qtd in Roberts, 1985, p. 24)

Against this backdrop Bond offers an uncompromising and savage exposure of the strategic imperative of violence. This is used not only by the old ruling class (Lear himself) but also by his daughters Fontanelle and Bodice after they have ousted him from power. Most significantly violence is employed by Cordelia's forces to achieve and sustain revolutionary change.

The play had its premiere, produced by the English Stage Company, at the Royal Court Theatre on 29 September 1971, directed by William Gaskill. It featured the actor Harry Andrews in the play's title role. In a programme note for a production of *Lear* at the Liverpool Everyman Theatre in October 1975, Bond wrote:

> Shakespeare's *Lear* is usually seen as an image of high, territorial academic culture. The play is seen as a sublime action and the audience is expected to show the depth of their culture by the extent to which they penetrate its mysteries [...] But the social moral of Shakespeare's *Lear* is this: endure till in time the world will be made right. That's a dangerous moral for us. We have to have a culture that isn't an escape from the sordidness of society, the 'natural' sinfulness or violence of human nature, that isn't a way of learning how to endure our problems – but a way of solving them. (Qtd in Roberts, 1985, p. 25)

In Bond's deconstruction of Shakespeare's classic Jacobean tragedy, Cordelia is portrayed, not as Lear's youngest and compassionate daughter, but as 'a rural female Castro', as Bond described her. She is a young woman catapulted into radicalised political consciousness. Driven to action through her experience of being raped by the soldiers under the authority of the new regime established by Fontanelle and Bodice, Cordelia then leads her own revolutionary army against their regime. The daughters and their forces prove as oppressive and violent in their enforcement of state power as any means their father had previously employed.

In the opening scene of the play, Lear is inspecting the ongoing fortification and building of the wall. He discovers that a worker has accidentally killed, through exhaustion, another worker. Lear orders the accused to face a firing squad, pronouncing: 'He killed a workman on the wall. That alone makes him a traitor.' With this chilling logic born out of paranoiac hubris, Lear then explains the vision that, for him, ideologically and materially embodies the wall:

> LEAR I started this wall when I was young. I stopped my enemies in the field, but there were always more of them. How could we

ever be free? So I built this wall to keep our enemies out. My people will live behind this wall when I am dead [...] My wall will make you free. That's why the enemies on our borders – the Duke of Cornwall and the Duke of North – try to stop us building it. I won't ask him which he works for – they're both hand in glove. Have him shot. (*L*, pp. 3–4)

Crucially different from Shakespeare's *King Lear* is that *Lear*, from the beginning, questions the nature of political power and its execution. There is no implicit assumption that political and indeed tyrannical power is either 'natural' or 'inevitable', or that it carries any implicit moral authority. In *King Lear* there is an intrinsic if unspoken subtext of a social and cultural code which necessitates a morally correct expression of filial devotion to the father. Cordelia's implicit filial love has a value which, she argues, is more 'natural' in its resistance to the explicit, culturally coded rhetoric of her two sisters. She is punished accordingly. In Bond's play, Lear's two daughters' decision to marry his enemies is viewed by Lear as both politically naive and suicidal. The daughters countermand their father's order that the worker should be shot; they claim their future husbands' patriarchal authority for themselves. Lear responds: 'My enemies will not destroy my work! I gave my life to these people [...] now you've sold them to their enemies!' before himself shooting the worker.

Anticipating what he views as his daughters' treachery against him, Lear's long following speech employs Freudian imagery to denounce their motives and actions:

I knew it would come to this! I built my wall against you as well as my other enemies! [...] You have perverted lusts. They won't be satisfied. It *is* perverted to want your pleasure where it makes others suffer. I pity the men who share your beds. (*L*, p. 7)

This strong sense of displaced desire sublimated as the will-to-power through violence is explored further in Bond's mapping of the complex territory of the daughters' strategic motives. They are both intent on eliminating each other and also their respective husbands following their planned political coup against their father. Fontanelle first says in her soliloquy, 'When he gets on top of me I have to count to ten. That's long enough'; and Bodice in her own dramatic aside, reveals, 'He must prove himself a man before he plays with his soldiers. He'll fuss and try all night, but he won't be able to raise his standard.'

These signifiers of clitoral self-empowerment present a powerful rejection of the phallocentric intrusion of the symbolic 'father' in both Lear and their husbands. This anticipates and prefigures the complex dialectics of gender, desire and power in the construction of the reactionary iconic persona of the 'Iron Lady': Margaret Thatcher, elected to power eight years on from the play's premiere.

There is evidence also of these characters in the metaphorical function of their names. The bodice, of course, an undergarment worn traditionally by women in the West, restricts and constrains its wearer. Hidden from view and concerned to accentuate and control the female body to the controlling male gaze, it epitomises the 'invisibility' of these gender power relations. One might read this cultural dress item therefore as a potent expression of the patriarchal restraining of the female materially and metaphorically.

'Fontanelle' is the name given to the crevices or cracks in the skull of a newly born baby whose elasticity and movement are essential to the safe birth of the neonate into the world. There is a subliminal sense of the emerging meta-reality of Bond's concept of 'radical innocence' hovering above and within this name. Like her sister Bodice, Fontanelle also faces constraint and remodelling into the patriarchal strictures of an ideologically repressive reality. In the same way that the plasticity of the neonate skull must endure reshaping in order to enter and survive in the world it's born into, both Bodice and Fontanelle have endured the constrictions of their father's authority. It is an authority embodied on both the ideological and psychodynamic site.

Both of these sisters revisit an appalling revenge for the constraints and repressions inflicted upon them by their father. As Bond reflected in a notebook entry dated 24 June 1970: 'The daughters attack Lear for all he's deprived them of. But they put all of this in the abstract' (Bond, 2000c, p. 102). This is vividly conveyed in scene 4 of the play. Here they both authorise, witness and sadistically participate in the torture of Warrington, Lear's former senior councillor and advisor. The older, desperately vulnerable man provokes a totemic fetishised anger from the women. He is a ruptured embodiment of despised phallic power and the displaced, sepulchral after-image of their hated father. His political and psychodynamic destruction and savagely rendered impotence is authorised and choreographed by them. It is a scene of unbearable cruelty, morbidly enhanced by an underlying gallows humour and sense of the grotesque. Open to viewing as a projected misogynous fear of unrestrained female desire, Fontanelle initiates a retributive rage against Warrington-as-Father-as-patriarchy:

> FONTANELLE Do something! Don't let him get away with it. O Christ, why did I cut his tongue out? I want to hear him scream!
> SOLDIER A (*jerks Warrington's head up*) Look at 'is eyes, miss. Thass boney-fidey sufferin.
> FONTANELLE O yes, tears and blood. I wish my father was here. I wish he could see him. (*L*, p. 28)

Then having jumped on her victim's hands with the soldier, Fontanelle screams:

> Kill it! Kill him inside! Make him dead! Father! Father! I want to sit on his lungs!
> BODICE (*knits*) Plain, pearl, plain. She was just the same at school. (*L*, p. 28)

Convinced that their political prisoner might still inform upon them to Lear and his forces, Bodice plunges her knitting needles into his ears. She then announces to the soldier her orders to 'Take him out in a truck and let him loose. Let people know what happens when you try to help my father.' Their torturing of their enemy in complex psycho-political terms takes on an additionally chilling significance of *realpolitik* 'theatre' in the intimidating propaganda value of the destroyed enemy of the state. This sequence of unremitting and orgiastic violence towards Warrington is a potent and deeply disturbing example of what Bond referred to in this period as 'aggro-effects'. As Spencer discusses with characteristic acuity:

> *Lear*'s violence is motivated not by a desire to 'revitalise' the original, but a desire to change its effect – to reinterpret the meaning of Lear's suffering. (Spencer, 1992, p. 83)

Helen Dawson, reviewing the opening production of the play for *The Observer* in October 1971, remarked:

> It is unmistakably the work of a visionary craftsman [...] *Lear*, despite its unflinching brutality, is not a negative work. It is a poetic indictment of what, in Bond's view, is wrong with our world and our values. (Qtd in Roberts, 1985, p. 23)

There is also a kind of haunting but non-sentimental pathos of the suffering endured by the victim through the character of the ghost of the Gravedigger's Boy:

> Lear did not have to destroy his daughters' innocence, he does so only because he doesn't understand his situation [...] But I think he had to destroy the innocent boy. Some things were lost to us long ago as a species, but we all seem to have to live through part of the act of losing them. We have to learn to do this without guilt or rancour or callousness – or socialised morality. So Lear's ghost isn't one of the angry ghosts from *Early Morning*, but something different. (Bond, 1978, p. 12)

The ghost of the Gravedigger's Boy is a major and defining example of a Bond character as a material, ontological meta-presence of the suffering dead. He is located at a crucial dialectical interaction; he is simultaneously immanent yet self-reflexively 'transcendent'. By this I do not mean a literal phenomenological transcendence. That early modern and later, revived Gothic notion of the supernatural is translated in this context into a revolutionary reading of materiality, imagination – and history itself. The contingent meta-materiality of the Boy's mortality encounters Lear's ideologically constructed politicised materiality. Lear and the Boy radically and profoundly reflect each other's co-existent reality.

The character's death is signified as a random victim of state-sanctioned terror. Significantly, whilst the Boy demonstrates practical concern and help towards Lear in life, it is in death that the Boy embodies a deeper reality. The ghost of the Gravedigger's Boy functions as a kind of Fool to Bond's Lear as was the Fool to Shakespeare's traumatised former king. In *King Lear* the Fool disappears without account or return. In *Lear* there is no cathartic transcending of

suffering nor is there any posthumous peace waiting for the Ghost
or, ultimately, Lear.

The character of the Gravedigger's Boy appears initially in Act 1
scene 5 when he takes pity on Lear after he has been left alone by
the Old Councillor (Warrington). This character is a former aide to
Lear intent on saving his own life by informing the sisters of Lear's
whereabouts. The Boy's wife (Cordelia) is frightened that her husband's compassion for the fugitive Lear will put their own lives at
risk. As she later tells Lear after she has come to power:

> CORDELIA You were here when they killed my husband. I watched
> them kill him. I covered my face with my hands, but my fingers
> opened so I watched. I didn't miss anything. I watched and I said
> we won't be at the mercy of brutes anymore we'll live a new life
> and help one another. The government's creating that new life – you
> must stop speaking against us. (*L*, p. 83)

As Patricia Hern helpfully notes in her commentary on *Lear*:

> The soldier's violation of her home and of herself forces her to act
> politically; it is not enough simply to endure. Shakespeare's hero-
> ine is defeated and hanged in her cell; Bond's revolutionary leader
> becomes hardened [...] through the exercise of power, driving oth-
> ers into political action against her. (Bond, 1983, p. xxxii)

In a notebook entry dated 25 March 1984, Bond wrote:

> Revolutions have always mobilised for a simple but urgent need:
> for bread, for land, for release from the threat of prison and pun-
> ishment. Yet the profounder aim of all revolution – and this is said
> after the first battles have been won but the apparatus of the old
> state still flourishes – is to change people. If this is only a secondary
> aim then the fulfillment of those basic needs under which revolu-
> tions mobilised will prevent this aim becoming a revolutionary
> demand. (Bond, 2001, p. 194)

In *Lear* we see Bond wrestling with the challenge of defining the
means by which people and their society might be radically changed.
This is in dialectical tension with the awareness expressed through

Lear's speech of traumatised self-awakening. Bond explores the ways in which externalised political change is informed by an 'internalised' ontological, psycho-dramatic revolutionising of consciousness.

In this important sense, the character of the ghost of the Gravedigger's Boy is a complex, poetic materialisation of the juncture between thesis and antithesis as the pathos of history. The two seemingly separate entities of the materiality of history and a radical, reflexive imaginative materiality are realised as one dialectically dramatised site. This is not of course 'pathos' in terms of Aristotelian, cathartic tragedy. Neither is 'history' in this context a crudely defined, externalised determinism separate from human agency. The quasi-messianic inevitability of history as Hegelian 'World Spirit' or in its Marxist-developed form as the 'dictatorship of the proletariat' is also implicitly critiqued.

The Ghost is a continuous reminder, not only to Lear but also to the audience, of the human cost of violence and specifically of political violence, in both its reactionary and revolutionary forms. He is the voice of those silenced by political repression. He is the visible face of those political activists executed and rendered invisible by totalitarian regimes such as the 'Disappeared' of Pinochet's Chilean neo-fascist force in the 1970s.

It is with profound resonance therefore that it is the Ghost who is with Lear in political confinement. Lear confesses to the Ghost: 'I shouldn't have looked. I killed so many people and never looked at one of their faces' (*L*, p. 56). The Ghost pleads with Lear to be allowed to stay with him in his prison cell:

> Let me stay with you, Lear. When I died I went somewhere. I don't know where it was. I waited and nothing happened. And then I started to rot, like a body in the ground [...] Are you afraid to touch me? (*L*, p. 56)

The two characters, both agents and victims of history and its political turmoil and tumult, close Act 2 scene 2. They inhabit a mutual vulnerability and shared humanity:

> LEAR Yes, yes, poor boy. Lie down by me. Here. I'll hold you. We'll help each other. Cry while I sleep, and I'll cry and watch you while you sleep. We'll take turns. The sound of the human voice will comfort us. (*L*, p. 56)

Act 2 scene 1 of the play is set in a courtroom where Lear is to face the equivalent of a war crimes trial at the instigation of his two daughters. These are categorically not intended to have a spurious or gratuitous 'shock effect' in themselves but are rather a visceral and dramatic exposure of a more deeply seated violence in human beings and society:

> It is for these reasons I say that society is held together by the aggression it creates, and men are not dangerously aggressive but our sort of society is. It creates aggression in these ways: first, it is basically unjust, and second it makes people live unnatural lives – both things which create a natural, biological aggressive response in the members of our society. Society's formal answer to this is socialised morality; but this, as I have explained, is only a form of violence, and so it must itself provoke more aggression. (Bond, 1978, pp. 8–9)

Evoking the *realpolitik* of the twentieth century from the former KGB Lubyanka prison in Moscow through to MI6 interrogations at Long Kesh prison in Belfast, this scene opens with a short framing dialogue between Bodice and the Judge:

> BODICE You've studied your instructions?
> JUDGE Indeed, ma'am.
> BODICE This is a political trial: politics is the highest form of justice. The old king's mad and it's dangerous to let him live. Family sentiment doesn't cloud our judgment. I've arranged to call the people who upset him most.
> FONTANELLE I'm a witness.
> BODICE Let him rattle on and condemn himself. Goad him if it helps – but not too openly.
> JUDGE I understand ma'am. (*L*, p. 46)

This scene is crucial to the dramatic and narrative strategies of the play. It is the point at which Lear undergoes a radical transformation in his own self-awareness and understanding. In this scene Bond also gives Lear some of the most powerful and moving speeches in the play. Bodice orders that her father be given her mirror in order that he might be tormented by his own pitiful condition. However, Lear is well aware from his own time in power that the supposed 'justice' of the proceedings against him barely masks the 'show trial' that it actually is. He shouts at the Judge: 'You have no right to sit there!' and when the Judge insists that Lear 'Take the oath', Lear retaliates with: 'I gave you your job because you were corrupt!' Insisting once more that Lear take an oath of effective collusion with the charade that will lead to his ultimate execution, Lear responds: 'The king is always on oath!' (*L*, p. 46).

This exchange frames Lear's subsequent speech. In Shakespeare's play Lear descends into a madness that is transformed into a cathartic sanity. In Bond's play Lear's madness is driven significantly and directly by a primordial encounter with himself. The encounter however is located on both a psycho-dynamic and an ideological site. It is a traumatic but liberating self-interrogation. Furthermore the internalised nature of the encounter is inseparable from its clear political context. The internal and external realities are symbiotic and co-symptomatic. Whereas Shakespeare's Lear suffers the tragic consequences initiated by an externalised Fate expressed through his hubris, Bond's equivalent is located on a more complex, modernist political site. This journey is not travelled in a simplistic, reductive form of an Ibsen-esque individualised psychological revelation. Instead, in a way that critically prefigures the deepening concerns of Bond's 'later plays' 30 years on from *Lear*, the revolutionising of Lear's consciousness is ontological, yet with inescapably political consequences. Shakespeare's Lear is pursued by a form of Fate and by the Furies consistent with those originating in classical culture and mythology. In Bond's *Lear* the Furies have assumed a more human form: that of daughters and the politically oppressed. One can therefore see a major landmark in the evolution of Bond's ongoing philosophical and dramatic thinking.

Bond employs a dark, complex, textured dramaturgy that is effectively sensual and visceral in its imagery and power. As Lear stares down into the mirror he expresses what develops into a litany of despair and horror:

> LEAR No, that's not the king [...] This is a little cage of bars with an animal in it. (*Peers closer*) No, no, that's not the king! (*Suddenly gestures violently. The* USHER *takes the mirror*) Who shut that animal

in that cage? Let it out. Have you seen its face behind the bars? (*L*, p. 49)

The speech is saturated with vivid imagery. With 'blood' and 'tears', Lear is 'broken', 'shocked, 'cut' and 'shaking' as he encounters himself in a cruel tapestry of dark materiality – a materiality which embodies its own simultaneous, nightmarish poetics:

> There's a poor animal with blood on its head and tears running down its face. Who did that to it? Is it a bird or a horse? It's lying in the dust and its wings are broken. Who broke its wings? Who cut off its hands so that it can't shake the bars [...] Who shut that animal in a glass cage? O god, there's no pity in this world. (*L*, p. 49)

Dehumanised and brutally objectified into a pitiful animalistic state, Lear's re-envisioning of himself evokes associations of the victims of the Nazi concentration camps. There are also evocations of the 'crucifix-creatures' in some of the immediate post-war paintings of Francis Bacon and Graham Sutherland.

The speech concludes with the most moving and disturbing identification of Lear with his unconscious in an explosive expression of tortured empathy and compassion:

> It's shocked and cut and shaking and licking the blood on its sides. (USHER *again takes the mirror from* LEAR) No, no! Where are they taking it now! Not out of my sight! What will they do to it! O god, give it to me! Let me hold it and stroke it and wipe its blood! (*L*, p. 49)

Bodice then intervenes to take the mirror from the Usher, explaining with vindictive, premeditated control, 'I'll polish it every day and see it's not cracked.' In the act of sustaining and preserving the mirror's use value she subtextually conflates the enhancement of surface (polish) and stability (not cracked) with the mirror's darkly dialectical symbolic value. By preserving the mirror in its use value to frame, control and 'reflect' reality, Bodice also empowers it with a sexualised allure of limpid, elusive 'surface'. This delineates her own desire, pleasured and corrupted through her sadistic denial of her father's political and psychic freedom. 'Yes,' she says, 'I've locked this animal in its cage and I will not let it out!'

In the penultimate scene of the play, Cordelia meets Lear, who has become a leading and articulate critic of her regime and consequently has attracted the interest and support of a growing number of citizens. Cordelia explains that she has come to speak with him because her revolutionary regime wants to put him on trial. When she asserts that there was no substantial difference between Lear and his two daughters who have been killed by her regime, he admits that this is so. 'You sound like the voice of my conscience,' she says. 'But if you listened to everything your conscience told you you'd go mad. You'd never get anything done – and there's a lot to do, some of it very hard' (*L*, pp. 97–8).

The ghost of her husband longs for a contact with or recognition from her which is as impossible as the ritual of *The Pope's Wedding*. He embodies the endless reverberation of those destroyed by violence through historical political struggle. Lear challenges Cordelia about the seeds of reaction already bearing a first and cancerous fruit in her commitment to retain and reinforce the wall. This is of course the same wall witnessed in the opening scene of the play. It acts as a material and metaphorical meta-frame to the dramatic action. In its dramatic significance and construction the wall exhibits a dialectic conjuncture and paradox. Its two surfaces *as* a wall are simultaneously interior and exterior. In their interiorised formation lies the false logic of containment-as-freedom. In their exteriorised surface lies the dialectical equivalence of defence-as-deterrence. Lear's disruption of the ideological and the materialist semiotics of the wall is a gesture of revolutionary intent and potential. His action which provokes his death challenges and explodes the repressive paradoxical myth of violence having an ideological, moral imperative to liberate and repress. Lear's action also embodies a paradox: only by choosing death can his liberation be achieved. In that death, it is not only the ideological and semiotic contradictions of the wall's semiotic that is exposed. It is also the revelation of the deeper meanings readable within Bond's construction of Lear. In that reading of the dramatic events the Ghost can also be read as a metaphor and material embodiment of Lear's repressed shadow self. In that sense the Ghost signifies that 'conscience which doth make liars of us all'. He embodies a radical, humanist counter-narrative to the injustice and cruel oppression of Lear's original regime. He simultaneously anticipates Lear's own final revolutionary action. This will bring Lear and the Ghost into a radicalised thesis of mortality. In it lies the fragile

possibility of a subsequent revolutionary history not reliant upon violence for its realisation and consolidation:

> GHOST Tell her I'm here. Make her talk about me.
> LEAR Don't build the wall.
> CORDELIA We must.
> LEAR Then nothing's changed! A revolution must at least reform!
> CORDELIA Everything *else* is changed!
> LEAR Not if you keep the wall! Pull it down!
> CORDELIA We'd be attacked by our enemies!
> LEAR The wall will destroy you. It's already doing it. How can I
> make you see?
> GHOST Tell her I'm here. Tell her. (*L*, p. 98)

Lear makes one final, impassioned attempt to make her change her
mind:

> Listen, Cordelia. If a god had made the world, might would always
> be right, that would be so wise, we'd be spared so much suffering.
> But we made the world out of our smallness and weakness. Our
> lives are awkward and fragile and we have only one thing to keep
> us sane: pity, and the man without pity is mad. (*L*, p. 98)

Lear's digging away of the wall remains one of the iconic, dramatic
moments from not only post-war but twentieth-century British
drama. Lear's action remains a capital offence as it was under his
own regime. He is watched by an officer, formerly the Farmer's Son
and compatriot of Cordelia, who aims his pistol in warning to Lear:

> LEAR (*spits on his hands and grips the shovel*) I'm not as fit as I was. I
> can still make my mark.

> LEAR *digs the shovel into the earth. The* FARMER'S SON *fires.* LEAR *is
> killed instantly.* (*L*, p. 102)

Lear's death is neither poetic nor tragic in the conventional senses of
those terms. From Bond's view, Lear's death is a rational consequence
in which the character accepts responsibility for his life and action,

as he wrote in the 1975 programme note: 'My Lear's gesture mustn't be seen as final. Lear is very old and has to die anyway. He makes his gesture only to those who are learning how to live' (qtd in Roberts, 1985, p. 25).

Edward Bond's *Lear* is one of the major plays of post-war and twentieth-century British theatre. Written and produced as it was at the beginning of a decade that was to conclude with the election of Margaret Thatcher's right-wing government, the play's revolutionary politics might be seen to occupy a distant land almost beyond view. It lies beyond a wall built by Thatcherism and as seemingly impregnable as that built by Lear and consolidated by Cordelia. It was and remains a wall built in order to support and rationalise the ruthlessly cynical, ruinous dismantling of the state. Its bricks and mortar are a vicious, right-wing ideological vested self-interest.

It is my view that disappointingly so much of recent contemporary theatre fails to engage in an explicit and clear debate and interrogation of the political and economic crisis facing our world. It is arguable that this reluctance reflects a failure to understand and therefore investigate the deeper, systemic failures and contradictions within early twenty-first-century capitalism.

In a review of the Royal Shakespeare Company's revival of *Lear* in 1983, Anthony Masters wrote in *The Times* on 21 May 1983:

> What is unbearable about seeing Edward Bond's greatest (and biggest) play again, twelve years after its Royal Court premiere, is not the horrors and bleakness of war, the mutilations ... and the other brutalities that had members of Thursday night's audience carried out in seizures of shock [...] It is the knowledge that it is even more topical now and will become more so as man's inhumanity gains subtle sophistication with the twenty-first century's approach. (Qtd in Roberts, 1985, p. 24)

In the intervening 30-odd years, the catalogue of 'man's inhumanity' has continued into the twenty-first century through Srebrenica in the former Yugoslavia to Baghdad, Helmand and Damascus.

In Bond's next major play following on from *Lear* he sought to investigate and expose the political and moral 'deep structural corruption of capitalist culture'.

Bingo: Scenes of Money and Death (1973)

In contrast to the way in which Bond radically deconstructs the 'mythic' status of Shakespeare's masterpiece in *Lear*, in *Bingo* it is the dominant cultural icon of Shakespeare as a writer that Bond investigates. *Lear* examined with rigorous clarity the tragic conundrums of political conflict and repression at a time of the Cold War and the Berlin Wall, the war in Ireland and a decade of mass Left political activism. *Bingo* focuses upon the relationship and the political and ethical responsibilities between a writer and his society. The context for Bond's play is the late Elizabethan and early Jacobean society, in which an economic revolution is in its dynamic early stages. It is driven by a powerful authoritarian political system and anticipates the onset of early capitalism and also, with some acuity, the emergence of the Thatcherite project of privatisation post-1979. The play's subtitle, *Scenes of Money and Death*, acts as a kind of schematic 'gestus' of the play's underlying themes and concerns.

Bingo was written in the same year as its first production at the Northcott Theatre, Exeter, on 14 November 1973, featuring Bob Peck as the protagonist, Shakespeare himself. It transferred to the Royal Court Theatre on 14 August 1974, with John Gielgud taking on the role of Shakespeare. Bond also offers additional insight into his thinking regarding the subtitle from first-draft notes:

> In what sense is money associated with death? What is the relationship between bread, or if you like, money, and love. Unless you feed, you cannot love. In *Bingo* money always leads to death. (Qtd in Hay and Roberts, 1980, p. 198)

This dialectical interplay is furthered and served by Bond's structuring of *Bingo*, which reveals the ethical dilemmas and ideological contradictions faced by Shakespeare within the play.

Early seventeenth-century England was a place and time of imperialist expansionism, in both Ireland and the New World. It was a monarchical society which traced its origins to the political and social structures imposed in the post-Norman Conquest period and later consolidated through the Plantagenet and Tudor dynasties and land-owning aristocracy. It was experiencing a radical transitional period with its economic base facing massive and potentially destabilising social and cultural change – not only 'foreigners' were perceived and manufactured as a 'threat', but also an increasingly large number of rootless and wandering poor. Their suffering and plight are critiqued by Bond, and encapsulated in the character of the Beggar Woman in *Bingo*. The destitute classes were viewed within the rationale of capitalism as an 'acceptable' and 'inevitable' consequence of 'reform' and productive efficiency, driven by the enclosure of common land and increase of privatised cash profit.

Bond employs his episodic scene structure to expose the potentially devastating contradictions inherent within the rationale of embryonic capitalism. His Shakespeare is seen as a writer and individual who is complicit with and within those structures, as a result of the commercial success of his plays. Having made a financially shrewd investment in the popular theatres that produced those plays, he has become a wealthy bourgeois. Facing the end of his working life, he has bought a country property near Stratford-upon-Avon to live out his retirement. Nevertheless Bond does not indulge in a reductive and critical caricaturing of Shakespeare as inherently or deliberately corrupt or cynically complicit. The interface between individualised consciousness and action and the values and power structures of a given society is both clear and yet complex. It might therefore be more accurate to view Bond's construction of Shakespeare as a symptom of a socio-political corruption. Like a diseased body, there is a disturbing symbiosis between host, disease and victim, with each re-infecting and re-enforcing the other. In Shakespeare's ultimate decision to commit suicide in the final scene of the play, Bond reveals the destructive consequences of this terminal socio-political condition for the individuals it infects.

There are plans for enclosure of the common land, and active and organised resistance to it by armed groups of peasants, personified particularly by the character of the Son – a young man whose mother is Shakespeare's housekeeper. Out of this ongoing violent resistance, the Son's father is eventually killed on the snow-driven heath above and beyond Shakespeare's home (explored further, later in this section). In reflecting upon the ethical and political contradictions confronting Shakespeare, Bond was arguably re-evaluating his own relationship to British society at the time. This necessitated Bond's forensic examination of the enduring political inequalities, injustices and violent oppressions of the twentieth century as a whole:

> SHAKESPEARE What does it cost to stay alive? I'm stupefied at the suffering I've seen. The shapes huddled in misery that twitch away when you step over them. Women with shopping bags stepping over puddles of blood. What it costs to starve people. The chatter of those who hand over prisoners. The smile of the men who see no further than the end of a knife. Stupefied. How can I go back to that? What can I do there? I talk to myself now. I know no one will ever listen. (*B*, p. 40)

This speech is given enhanced power in the context of where it occurs in the play. Shakespeare has walked up onto the hills beyond Stratford and his home. Effectively crucified by Combe as an agent of a repressive, authoritarian state, the dead and decomposing body of the Beggar Woman stares out across the world. That world has punished her for her class and gender and alleged transgression through public execution. She had entered Shakespeare's garden in the opening scene of the play. The first location conveyed a deceptive oasis of calm and meditative retreat from the world. With subtle dramatic economy and powerful tragic irony in terms of her ultimate fate, she embodies the commodification of the human. In terms of the market criteria of supply and need, she has consented to have paid sex in return for a cash payment from the Old Man, Shakespeare's gardener and husband to his housekeeper. Prior to this, Shakespeare has discovered her presence on his property and offered her food which she has refused in preference for money. He also asks the Old Woman (his housekeeper) if there might not be 'cast-off' clothes from his wife to provide clean clothes for the itinerant traveller. In this action, happening arguably in a subconscious as well as a social location, the Beggar Woman is to be offered the discarded clothes of Shakespeare's daughter or wife. If the manufactured materiality of clothes might be viewed as equivalent to the socio-cultural ideological 'dressing' of female identity, the Beggar Woman has her need 're-dressed'. In this, patriarchy affords her a provisional equivalence with the other women, regardless of their difference in social class and status. The poor and marginalised don't of course need the surplus-to-requirement cast-offs of the bourgeoisie to 'redress' their exploited position.

However, the Beggar Woman understands something far more immediate and pertinent to both her oppressed condition and her means
of survival. She recognises the dynamic implications of the power
of money, and its invidious corruption of everything it touches.
Through the harsh unyielding oppression of poverty and her life
on the streets she knows that money has a perversely 'transcendent'
value far beyond food. This is central to the 'currency' (or value) of
'currency' within capitalism's economic *modus operandi*. Capitalism
identifies and produces a commodity-value of bread or a woman's
body. Through the interface of profit margins and labour costs
it establishes the differential between production costs and sale/
exchange value.

In *Bingo*, the characterisation of women is interesting. It is important to note the one female character that the audience never sees
is that of Shakespeare's wife. Referred to at intervals throughout the
play, her character is associated with an actual and metaphorical
invisibility. This 'disappeared female presence' is conspicuous by its
absence and carries with it connotations of her debilitating ill health.
Through carefully nuanced subtextual allusions, the cause of her
suffering seems to be as much emotional and psychological as it is
physical. In a telling way her material visibility is conveyed through
the angry neurosis and avid self-interest of Judith, Shakespeare's
daughter. She is bitterly critical of her father and consumed with
anger towards him. She views with a quiet rage what she sees as his
indolence. This is conflated in her view with what she perceives and
resents as his moral arrogance and detachment. This detachment,
she believes, is his chosen method of avoiding contact or purposeful
action with the demands of the world. It is all expressed and conveyed in her cry: 'She doesn't know who she is, or what she's supposed to do, or who she married. She's bewildered – like so many of
us!' (*B*, p. 32), referring specifically to herself and her mother.

The Beggar Woman is arrested in Shakespeare's orchard having
been seen by the Son in her postcoital liaison with the Old Man,
his father. Significantly it is Judith who, in opposition to both
her father and the Old Woman, sides with Combe's judgemental,
punitive stance. The Beggar Woman is to be arrested and taken to
the town square for a public whipping. When the Beggar Woman
cries out for mercy, Combe tells her: 'If there's something wrong
with your head it'll do it good. Doctors whip mad people' (*B*, p. 23).

Judith's reactionary moral position places her in ideological collusion with Combe and the land-owning patriarchy. She feels profoundly denied of recognition and social and moral volition by her father's psychological distance. In the proactive economic adventurism of Combe she perceives an inspirational model of self-empowerment. Through this, her own desire for recognition might be awakened and addressed. This might also be read as a form of a displaced sexual desire expressed as an alienated form of clitoral self-empowerment. Identifying with the powerful imbues even the socially and culturally diminished with a projected participation in that power. Judith is denied individual self-determination and expression by the social and cultural codes of power in Jacobean society. Therefore in order to navigate a strategy of relative empowerment under those repressive restrictions, this necessitates her identification with the dominant male presence.

From this reading of her behaviour and actions, her anger against her father embodies a dual, subconscious function. Judith resents her father for denying her 'visibility' and a 'voice' which simultaneously locks her into the same position as her mother. We might also read her anger as being aimed at what she sees as her father's symbolic 'impotence', the self-same (symbolic) Father who denies her voice and visibility as a woman in the social and cultural sphere. Shakespeare also offers Judith no means of (symbolic) psycho-sexual consummation through his impotent failure to intervene in the world of 'money and death'. Judith's identification with Combe and his patriarchal power may be viewed as a complex displacement strategy for quasi-empowerment and recognition. This is not, however, to suggest that the displacement activity is narrowly or simplistically aligned to the penetrative strategies of emerging venture capitalism. The character of Judith is a compelling example and prefiguring of what would emerge from 1979 onwards as the paradox of a Thatcherite female identity. Judith's existential unease as a woman signifies the collision of a woman seeking to exert proactive agency in a patriarchal society. In this she embodies a contradiction that perversely undermines yet empowers her as a woman. In order to escape her fear of being destined to be dressed in the invisibility of her mother, she must don the cloak of patriarchal visibility. What kind of a fit could that be? As oppressively ill-fitting as the uniform that Bond had been forced to wear in his national service?

The wearing of clothing that signals a metaphorical and ideological materiality can be traced back of course to Scopey in *The Pope's Wedding*. It is also present in the play *Jackets*. In *Red Black and Ignorant* from *The War Plays* trilogy we find a scene in which the Mother helps fit her Son into his uniform before he leaves to kill an innocent man. Giving a grimly ironic dimension to the expression 'dressed to kill', this is given deeper resonance when the Son ultimately chooses to kill his father rather than a vulnerable old neighbour. Judith, in *Bingo*, is as trapped within a paradox as impossible and irreconcilable as Scopey is. And this same phenomenon is seen again in one of Bond's later, post-2000, plays, *The Edge*. In this play, the character of the older man slowly and silently dresses in the clothes which he has stolen out of the rucksack of the young man. Judith's relationship with Combe is further complicated in terms of gender politics by her simultaneous if implicit support of the Son's fundamentalist Christian denouncement of the Beggar Woman and his father.

From a broadly Marxist reading of the relationship between the economic base of nascent seventeenth-century capitalism and its social and cultural superstructure, one can interpret the extent to which all of the characters are enmeshed in the strictures of money and its acquisition. One of the significant achievements of *Bingo* is the way in which Bond is able to retain a proper critical distance in the construction of his characters and their interrelationship. The extent to which their identities and motives are located within a social, economic and effectively a cash nexus exudes a transparent clarity. This defines and conveys the characters beyond the limiting reductive Brechtian constraints of simply ciphers of historical determinism. This is especially evident in the complex layering of the socio-political external and psychological internal in Bond's construction of Shakespeare. Bond's Shakespeare is much more than a means by which the past can be radically revisited and deconstructed. The play seeks to explore and achieve more than the identification of prime historical suspects for the political and economic parallels escalating through the 1970s. In that important sense Bond is far more interested in the latent existential and even ontological strata of human existence, imagination and society.

Bond achieves this in *Bingo* through his recognition that Shakespeare's dramatic imagination is not entirely a symptom of class consciousness. Neither is it an innately subjective phenomenon in a post-Romantic understanding of the artist and the visionary imagination. Scholars such as Reinelt assert that:

> He [Bond] always historicises the incidents of the narrative, providing a representation of the social construction of the subject, in scenes with a clear political gestus. (Reinelt, 1996, p. 51)

Nevertheless I believe this reading is rather limited in that it insufficiently acknowledges the primacy of a different form of revolutionary imagination in Bond's writing and dramatic vision. Bond interrogates this territory:

> Imagination is more logical than pure reason because it is embodied: it does not need proof [...] Justice is created by material acts not by desires in the imagination. Imagination seeks reason and understanding. This makes it vulnerable to social madness [...] Art is not transcendental – nothing is. If art is to free some, it must be possible for it to drive others deeper into corruption. (Bond, 2000b, pp. 168–9)

Bond's Shakespeare is a writer whose engagement with the society and world in which he lives is characterised by a traumatic rupture of his imagination. This has been provoked by the suffering he witnesses, caused by social and political injustice. By this I don't mean that the ethical and ideological faultline is in an essentialist sense 'within' Shakespeare's creative imagination – this would wrongly reinforce a concept of the disembodied, abstracted imagination of a neo-Romantic variety. It is rather two things. The first is that, as Bond observed, 'Shakespeare's plays show this need for sanity and its political expression, justice [... but] His behaviour as a property owner made him closer to Goneril than to Lear' (*B*, p. 6). This does not preclude for the character human compassion or pity. It does entail a potentially overwhelming realisation that 'Justice is created by material acts not by desires in the imagination.' Secondly, such a realisation makes Shakespeare 'vulnerable to social madness'. If art can offer no cathartic or quasi-transcendent purpose, it can only function in an embodied, materialist form and function. For Shakespeare it is only through suicide that an alternative ethical system enters human social reality. As Shakespeare stands in front of the decaying, crucified body of the executed Beggar Woman, her fetishised body signals the brutal authoritarianism of Jacobean law whilst exposing its inherent denial of human justice. Shakespeare's subsequent monologue conflates her suffering with that of the non-human animal-victim of the popular cultural bear-baiting yards:

> Flesh and blood. Strips of skin. Teeth scrapping bone [...] Men baiting their beast [...] And later the bear raises its great arm. The paw with a broken razor [...] It looks as if it's making a gesture to the crowd. Asking for one sign of grace, one no. And the crowd roars, for more blood, more pain, more beasts huddled together, tearing flesh and treading in living blood. (*B*, p. 39)

The logic of Shakespeare's imagination and its desire for justice and compassion is subverted by the material realities of Elizabethan and Jacobean society. It evokes comparisons with Lear's traumatic mirrored self-realisation as a form of victimised and oppressed beast. Bond's Shakespeare faces existential meltdown and mental collapse as he endeavours to reconcile the irreconcilable. This scenario embodies and constitutes the brutal social, economic and political contradictions of his society. Shakespeare as a writer, like Lear as a deposed tyrant, glimpses a potentially revolutionary and transformative course of action. It is through the dialectic between his radical imagination and his growing awareness of those destructive external conditions that Shakespeare chooses suicide as an existentially radical and morally revolutionary act. In this context, as Bond proceeded to assert in his essay, 'You may recognise others only when you can recognise yourself. In drama this is possible – in drama we may meet and recognise ourselves in the gap' (Bond, 2000b, p. 169).

This 'gap' is not the transcendent in any usual or conventional use of that term as Shakespeare mordantly reflects as he stands before the executed woman. It may however be read as a paradigmatic expression of how human beings may know themselves and know one another more truly through drama. The materiality of the imagination is facilitated and revealed by the 'external' materiality of dramatic action. This 'theatre event' is rather a harrowing icon of all of history's persecuted victims through Auschwitz to the Bosnian War's Srebrenica:

> There's no higher wisdom of silence. No face brooding over the water. No hand leading the waves to the shore as if it's saving a dog from the sea [...] No other hand ... no face ... just these. (*B*, p. 40)

Imagination cannot in and of itself be or constitute transcendence. There is no *deus ex machina*, no 'face brooding over the water'. Nevertheless the nature and means of the imagination to re-vision our humanity can help contribute to the conditions for building a society based upon justice and compassion. The revolutionised human imagination affords itself a critical and ethical viewing frame, and from this perspective, transformative, revolutionary action can intervene in and change the world. Imagination in this crucial sense possesses and exhibits its own distinctive, interventionist materiality. This then simultaneously impacts upon the enmeshed material realities of human history and the natural universe. As Bond explains:

> What would it be like if everything in the material world stopped, caught in one instant? We would be imprisoned in it. But the imagination is always caught in the present, stopped, trapped. We are imprisoned in the imagination. Yet it is the source of our humanness – and to create our humanness we must be free. So we must secure an exit for our imagination: we do this by putting it on the stage [...] In our present wounded state it is exhausting to be human. But we may endure it long enough to appear to ourself in the gap. That is why we need tragedy. (Bond, 2000b, pp. 168–9)

This 'gap' is the juncture between Shakespeare's and, by implication, Bond the writer's own immersion in the materiality of the world. In that gap is provided the revelation that their imaginative intervention makes possible in that enlightened moment of the caught present. The gap signifies the dialectic between the externalised material reality and its radicalised, transformative perception. The radicalised imagination is the gap that *is* no gap: the disruption of the spectacle and the apperception of the real. Through that radicalised perception achieved by the transformative imagination we reach the concept developed by Bond of the revolutionary imperative of the 'Internalised Transcendent'.

It is in this parallel context that Bond's Shakespeare finds a devastatingly clear self-knowledge that is equally a truer view of the social, economic, political and cultural corruption of his society: 'To have usurped the place of God, and lied' (*B*, p. 41).

Shakespeare is like someone who wakes like a sleepwalker might to suddenly and traumatically see the truth about himself and his world. However, he has no means by which to wake others other

than through his writing. This is compromised by his partial collusion with the forces of oppression. What this constitutes is an existential and ontological hell of alienated identity: the voiceless-voice.
He is haunted by his guilt-induced impotency of 'Was anything
done?' (his last line in the play). In a strange postmodern evocation
of the historical Shakespeare with his reimagined fictionalised dramatic self, Bond's character is effectively confronted by what Bond in
interview with this author referred to as the 'Hamlet colon': 'To be:
or not to be?' (Qtd in Billingham, 2007, p. 3):

> SHAKESPEARE I howled when they suffered, but they were whipped
> and hanged so that I could be free. That is the right question: not
> why did I sign one piece of paper? (*B*, pp. 62–3)

Like Lear, Bond's Shakespeare ultimately takes his own life. Like his
fictional predecessor, Shakespeare's action should not be seen entirely
or principally as an act of despair. It is not a gesture of nihilistic res-
ignation, rather it is a profound attempt to exercise and implement
a moral choice, and in doing so it exposes the corrupt conflation
of public morality with the cash nexus allied to an authoritarian
patriarchy.

Shakespeare's relationship with the land is one with clear ethical
implications. In his knowing or unwitting collusion with Combe
and the political and commercial establishment, Shakespeare himself
becomes a form of property. One might argue that the process of cultural and economic commoditisation reached its zenith with the various souvenir Shakespeare T-shirts, fridge magnets, etc. available in the
gift shop of the Royal Shakespeare Company in Stratford and beyond.

Shakespeare's plays have failed to change or substantially challenge that political and economic establishment any more than the
wider tranche of left-wing dramatists of the 1960s and 1970s helped
to achieve significant political change. Whilst Bond himself might
not subscribe to the world-weary pessimism of Trevor Griffiths' fictional, left-wing northern playwright Malcolm Sloman from his play
The Party (1973), he might endorse the implicit, uncompromising
honesty and political insight:

> The only thing you're allowed to put into the system is that
> which can be assimilated and absorbed by it [...] this is a society

that matured on descriptions of its inequity and injustice. Poverty is one of its best-favoured spectacles. Bad housing, class-divisive schools, plight of the sick and the aged, the alienating indignities of work, the fatuous vacuities of 'leisure' – Jesus God, man, we can't get enough of it. (Qtd in Billington, 2007, p. 213)

The relationship between the artist and society and the extent to which art and especially theatre can challenge, change and be part of a wider historical project of progressive transformation is even more questionable in the post-Thatcher and post-Blair period. High-cultural institutions such as the Royal Opera House, English National Opera, the National Theatre and the Royal Shakespeare Company find their budgets and institutionalised allegiance rewarded with protected budgets.

The historical Shakespeare was a canny and shrewd investor who profited from the commercial success of his plays. This success occurred through a popular public theatre culture that had flourished in his lifetime. Bond empowers his fictionalised Shakespeare to choose death as a radically self-reflexive moral critique. Bond arguably rescues the historical character from the existential and actual ditch where he lay, desperately drunk after a drinking bout with Ben Jonson. It is believed that he died soon after from his subsequent pneumonia and hypothermia.

As Bond's Shakespeare awaits his imminent death, having swallowed the tablet of poison given to him by Jonson, there is a truly disturbing parallel drama played out in the marginalised space of his daughter's and wife's material and psychological desperation. The stage direction reads:

> *Outside the two women bang on the door. The crying is louder and wilder. Suddenly it becomes hysterical* [...] *The door is violently banged, kicked and shaken. Someone scratches it. Outside the* OLD WOMAN *gasps and shrieks hysterically.* (B, pp. 60–1)

The rapacious clamour of the two women for the new will and testament that they fear he has written climaxes in the door being flung open and Judith ransacking the room. She is indifferent to her father who lies dying on the floor.

The Beggar Woman has lost her life and the Old Woman has lost her husband. Judith and her mother have lost a father and husband who, however alienated from them, was their sole material provider.

Shakespeare's suicide might therefore be read ultimately both as a symptom of terminal social, cultural and political conditions, and as the writer-as-physician belatedly acting to diagnose and remedy his morally terminal disease. Knowing that he has been culpable to its spread, he asks: 'Was anything done?' (*B*, p. 57).

It is not enough from Bond's perspective to assert that the past and its culturally iconic figures need to be radically deconstructed. Neither does he solely expose and liberate them from the dominant, meridian readings of their historical meaning and significance. Combe cynically and pragmatically observes to Shakespeare that 'Everyone listens to money' (*B*, p. 19). There is a mordant resonance between the ways in which the centrifugal power of money disempowers and effectively destroys other oppositional viewpoints. Money and death embrace each other like grotesques in a medieval Christian mural of Hell. They are locked in a dark dialectic of the faux-transcendence of surplus profit against the immanence of human mortality. Within the play these dialectics are characterised by the Beggar Woman and Shakespeare, who both recognise the primacy of money. Respectively, she chooses money over bread whilst he selects cash security against the risk of opposing the imminent juggernaut of enclosure and land clearance. The wider social, economic and political consequences lie in the attendant suffering and hardship for the poor. Crucially, what will also be brutally and unsentimentally swept away is the medieval, feudal dispensation of land and social and economic mutuality. Whilst this constituted a paternalistic and hierarchical system of rural social and economic organisation with an ethos of largesse (from surplus) by the land-owning rich and deferential dependence from the community, it did admittedly provide a degree of common, sustainable existence.

With the notable, if problematic, exceptions of theatre activists and companies such as Joan Littlewood at Stratford East and John McGrath's 7:84, there were very few, if any, sustained, left-radical interventions by theatre in the lives and communities of the British working class. In tangential connection with this, it is interesting that the sole encounter between Shakespeare and another writer in

Bingo is in scene 4 where Ben Jonson has arrived at Stratford. Jonson and Shakespeare become increasingly drunk and Jonson deliberately tries to provoke Shakespeare, asking 'What's your life been like? Any real blood?' (*B*, p. 45). Jonson's bitterness towards the world and his uncompromising exasperation with Shakespeare is focused principally on what he views as the latter's 'serenity'. By this Jonson refers to what he perceives as an impotent, self-preoccupied, even reactionary 'passivity' that characterises Shakespeare. As the two writers become increasingly inebriated it is with some dark and telling irony that they share the inn with a group of peasant 'political activists' led by the Son. They are sheltering from the snow storm that is rapidly raging outside having spent the evening digging up the enclosure ditches made by Combe's men. The contrast between those poor peasants taking action that would result in their execution if discovered and the bitter and resigned detachment of the two writers is telling. It encapsulates the wider political and cultural tensions between avowedly left-wing and progressive theatre and its failure to engage with and mobilise the working class throughout the period of the play.

In a scene made poignant by the child-like absorption of the Old Man with the intoxicating whiteness of the snow, he and Shakespeare enact a scene evocative of Lear and the Fool in Shakespeare's tragedy. They make and throw snowballs at each other. Their lapsing into an adult revisiting of a time of childhood playfulness and innocence signals momentarily as if it might be possible to escape the oppressions of human society.

When Shakespeare asks the Old Man if he has been up on the hill he responds with two evocative images of death – that of the Beggar Woman's corpse and a rabbit he has killed:

> OLD MAN [...] I saw the fields turn white. (*He laughs*) She had a little heap set top on her head. Like a cap. [...] You charm a rabbit by your play ... I grabs one an' broke his neck for'n. (*He holds out a dead rabbit*) Bad. Some'un elsen. (*B*, p. 54)

The two images are powerful. One is of the dead woman executed for trespass and the burning of barns in the battle of the enclosures; the other is of the dead rabbit with the old man's residual guilt about it being someone else's 'property'. The woman and the animal share a complex dialectic of death and the posthumous 'guilt' of property-value. One might say that there are also parallel semantic migrations of 'gilt' and 'guilt'. This guilt lies not in the actions of the Beggar Woman or the Old Man. It lies in the collective guilt confronting a society in which money and its ownership and production are predominant and 'bingo' really is 'the name of the game'.

The chimera of the snowball fight and its quasi-innocence is brutally extinguished shortly after the panic-driven running across of shadowy figures, a pistol shot and the subsequent death of the Old Man. It is significant that the victims of organised political activism in *Bingo* are a destitute woman and an old man. She was reduced to the most humiliating economics of trading her body for cash. He had been psychologically disabled in war through forced military conscription. There is equally a deeply unsettling and problematic absence of response to the fatal incident by Shakespeare himself.

In the final scene of *Bingo* the Son is alone with Shakespeare. Uttered with an unsettling calm, the Son nevertheless seeks to rationalise an action that is symbolically ambivalent in both political and filial terms:

> SON When yo' think on't, t'ent so sure I shot him neither. I fire a gun – I yont hide non truth. That yont mean I shot him. Someone else'n moight a fired. Death on an unarmed man – that's more loike the sort a thing Combe'd get up to. That want sortin' out in my yead. I may have done meself a wrong. (*B*, p. 65)

No clear revolutionary progress has been advanced but, like the ghost of the Gravedigger's Boy in *Lear*, the necessities of political struggle and resistance are calculated on the deaths of the poor and marginalised. The Old Man's relative innocence and vulnerability are expressed as a form of childhood through the conflation of the word 'boy' in connection to an adult man. Nevertheless it is a problematic and false innocence that had sentenced the Old Man to an exile in childhood caused by injuries sustained in warfare. The Old Woman offers a resigned if poignant eulogy for her dead husband to Shakespeare, who is about to face his own death:

> OLD WOMAN He'd bin t'see that dead woman, that's 'ow it ended. (*She shrugs*) He weren't greedy for money loike some men. I yont

know ... He wanted summat a child want. I yont know what. (*She shrugs*) Well, yo' break a cup yo' put it t'gither. Yont kip arskin' 'oo brok it. That's all as is. (*B*, p. 59)

The Fool: Scenes of Bread and Love (1975)

In *The Fool* Bond revisits the past once more in order to examine and expose the economic injustices of emerging capitalism. He further develops his critique of this model of economic organisation and the social and cultural systems that it engenders. In so doing he continues to mine a rich vein of historical, political and cultural strata that had begun with *Lear* and followed by *Bingo*. Significantly and directly after his critique and radical deconstruction of the dominant cultural icon of Shakespeare, Bond chose again to use a writer as a central focus. In the case of *The Fool*, however, it is not a writer synonymous with the dominant cultural and political establishment as with Shakespeare. Rather in the historical character of John Clare, Bond selected a writer much closer to his own class-based identity and indeed his broad geographical origins. It is not that this choice of location reflects a simplistic or reductive auto-biographical equivalence. More interestingly it is in the dramatic site of the play rather than the geographical location in which one sees a correspondence of class perspective and experience. Bond's Clare remains close to the nineteenth-century poet's rural and peasant roots, and social and economic background. The subtitle of the play, as in *Bingo*, evokes a kind of 'gestus' of the play's dominant political themes and concerns. John Clare was for most of his life on the exposed social and economic margins of English society. It was an era of political reaction and often brutal authoritarianism. The threat of revolution and the consequent overthrowing of the monarchy, aristocracy and Church as had happened in France had been consolidated by 'The Terror'. This had then been followed by the Imperial Republicanism of Bonaparte and a post-revolutionary, autocratic French state. This political background and its implications are referred to by the Parson and Lord Milton in the opening scene of the play. The Parson provides a homily to the peasants who have just performed a Christmas 'Mummers Play' for the lord and his guests, 'In this year of our lord eighteen hundred and fifteen England is beset by troubles.' Milton goes on to add that 'The war made us all prosperous but prices have fallen with the peace. Wages must follow. Not because I say so [...] Wages follow prices or civil institutions break down. Civilisation costs money like everything else' (*F*, p. 88).

Severe and consecutive harvest failures caused untold misery for many and especially the rural and rapidly growing urban poor. The growing clamour for political reform characterised by the Chartists and the related Peterloo Massacre of 1819 combine to create a world of overpowering oppression and suffering. As Bond stated in his original Introduction to the play:

> The last scene of *The Fool* is set in an asylum. In this scene I've tried to show that rational processes were still being worked out even in the apparently insane world of nineteenth-century Europe. The English slums of that time were like slow-motion concentration camps – death takes longer in slums than in concentration camps. Art has always looked at the atrocities of the age in which it was created. What Adorno and Auden said about poetry and Auschwitz misses the point. They would have hit it only if Auschwitz had been the summing up of history – and of course it wasn't. (Bond, 1987, p. 79)

The rural peasants in *The Fool* are 'close cousins' of the Son and his fellow peasant radicals in *Bingo*. However, the Son's radical religious, Millennial ideology which offered a problematic, 'higher' authority to his political struggle is denied Clare, Darkie and others in *The Fool*. Mid-seventeenth-century Millennial thinking shared certain similarities with the 'inevitable' ultimate victory intrinsic to a reductive, determinist Marxist reading of the 'dictatorship of the proletariat'. Sects such as the Levellers and Ranters, who were broadly synonymous with the historical setting of *Bingo*, advocated political and personal freedom in human social and sexual relationships. Related beliefs included the common ownership of all property and land. Equally from this oppositional viewpoint the rich and powerful embodied a corrupt 'Babylon' which would be overthrown by the 'Second Coming' of Christ. This 'saviour' nevertheless had everything in common with the poor and nothing in common with the rich and the powerful. From that ideological reading of human history, the Millennial groups saw themselves as an 'elect': a vanguard of the ultimate dialectic of history. From this perspective all individual actions are imbued with a metaphorically 'transcendent' value. In the same way, from a classical Marxist reading of history as political struggle, human actions and their consequences are justified and authorised by the overriding metaphor of historical necessity and justice. That value is the one consigned by the authority of history-as-destiny. It equates to the self-justifying rationale of the Son after he has killed his father.

For Darkie, Clare, Patty and the others in *The Fool* there is no 'transcendence' but only the rationale of the fundamental material necessities for food ('Bread' from the play's subtitle) and shelter. Their stripping and robbing of the Parson in scene 3 exhibits amongst other things the way in which religion had long ceased to serve as either a comfort or a form of political radicalism for the poor. In terms of the dramatic semiotics of this 'theatre event', the stripping away of the Parson's material possessions also demonstrates the challenging and taking of the ideological apparel of his role and status. When the Parson is finally naked, Darkie accusingly asks: 'Where you stole that flesh boy? Your flesh is stolen goods. You're covered in stolen goods when you strip? [...] You call us thief when we took silver. You took flesh!' (*F*, p. 106).

This proto-revolutionary encounter between Darkie and the other peasants with the Parson is traumatic for them all. The character Miles says in tears, 'O god o God how shall us ever git our things back. All the things they stolen' (*F*, p. 106). With additional semiotic and political significance, the bloodstained garment of the wounded character Lawrence is thrown to the Parson to cover his nakedness. Betty chastens the Parson for his bemoaning of his humiliation: 'You stood there two minute boy. I've made a mock of all my life' (*F*, p. 107). This climactic scene comes to a tragic conclusion for the peasant activists with the arrival of Lord Milton and his men and the fatal shooting of Lawrence. Just prior to this, Darkie bravely and uncompromisingly confronts Milton:

> DARKIE You steal from us. Parson steal from us. What we doo t'parson? Make a mock. Took – what? Trinkets! When I steal from parson what you doo t'me? Law hang us. Thass the on'y difference 'tween you an' me: you 'ont think twice 'fore you use violence. (*F*, p. 108)

In terms of the historical setting of *The Fool* there began in the eighteenth and early nineteenth centuries a rapid rise in anti-establishment, nonconformist denominations such as the Methodists. More exotically there were also sects such as that founded by the pseudo-savant Swedenborg with whom William Blake was briefly associated. Nevertheless, for the majority of the poor and oppressed underclass, belief in a God who embodied the possibility of any truly radical, progressive intervention in human affairs had failed and passed. It was not 'transcendence' that the poor needed but liberation through radical political change. From Darkie's perspective especially, this action lies solely in their own hands in direct terms and employing political violence if necessary. As Coult perceptively recognises:

> *The Fool* takes the dialectic between individual and collective sanity still further to show how the accumulated weight of a culture, its history, belief and social mores, press on and distort the individual personality [...] In *The Fool* Bond shows how a developing middle-class culture, the first shoots of modern capitalism, begin to whittle away at the living working-class culture that had been able to survive under feudalism. (Coult, 1977, p. 67)

Clare and Darkie represent dialectical and mutual oppositional attitudes and values within their shared class. As Bond asserted in a previously unpublished interview cited in Roberts:

> Clare is light, you see, and I deliberately chose the name Darkie – it's an invented name [...] Clare the poet, light, understanding, interpretation, and he doesn't want to use force because force [...] isn't to do with that side of human behaviour which is to do with kindness and generosity and so on. (Qtd in Roberts, 1985, p. 35)

The seemingly irreconcilable tensions between the necessity of revolutionary, even violent, political action, and the progressive political values necessary to inform that action, are a constant concern throughout many of Bond's plays and theoretical writings. Through his creative imagination and writer's response to his world, Clare, 'light', facilitates a vision for social and political change but lacks the direct-action power and means to realise it. Darkie, by comparison, understands the necessity of revolutionary action, enforced through violence if necessary, but struggles with a wider, coherent understanding to inform and enlighten it:

> Clare knows, for instance, that you can't change the world simply by smiling at it ... but if he uses just force ... all he will do is simply recreate the problem ... Clare is locked up in prison, just as Darkie's locked up in prison ... both their lives are wasted and that's simply because the two necessary parts of action – understanding and whatever force is necessary to put that understanding into effect – are not joined. (Bond qtd in Roberts, 1985, p. 36)

Darkie has only his market labour-value to support him whereas Clare has an additional, 'abstracted' value in his skills as a writer. Nevertheless as the play unfolds, it becomes clear that creativity and imagination in themselves offer no transcendent insights as political resolutions. Contemporary Romantic poets such as Wordsworth, the artisan-class Keats and aristocratic Shelley, by contrast, averred otherwise. Instead Clare himself becomes 'romanticised' and idealised by the aristocratic patronage of the ruling class and the neutering effect of the London, middle-class literary elite. He is constructed and viewed from this perspective as a 'Nature' poet. The concept of 'Nature' does not reflect the harsh Social Darwinism of Darkie and others. It is a reactionary fantasy of an English countryside idealised and utterly removed from the realities of rural life. A primitive precursor of the later, twentieth-century notion of cosmopolitan 'literary celebrity', John Clare's role and function as a writer become commoditised. Simultaneously he becomes disempowered and, with ultimately tragic consequences, insane. His social, cultural and ideological marginalisation destroys a writer who might have been an authentic, oppositional voice for the poor and dispossessed. The fate of both Clare and Darkie embodies the tensions and contradictions related to the dialectic of political violence and the role of art and the artist in revolutionary struggle. As Bond wrote in 1981 in relation to *Restoration*:

> Violent confrontation *is* inevitable if you are forced to live irrationally. Because it is the only way things will change [...]

We haven't yet found a way of change by using our minds. (Qtd in Roberts, 1985, p. 49)

Socially and culturally sanctioned violence characterises the fight between the two pugilists in the park and serves to present a critical 'viewing distance' of the fight as a paradigm of the very same socio-cultural elite who are 'betting' on Clare.

This is very much the case in *The Fool*, where there is effectively a dialectical relationship between the fight and Clare's conversation with the literati and London bourgeois class. The dramatic incidents 'speak' to each other. Significantly their language is decipherable in its principal function: to expose the hidden ideological forces at work beneath the social and cultural surface of the normative. In that sense the two incidents also exhibit in their paradoxical separateness their political, economic and cultural interconnectedness. The fight between the two working-class pugilists embodies the wider class struggle of the play's historical setting whilst also prefiguring the struggle between a paternalistic and patronising dominant culture which will ultimately destroy Clare.

The violence of the fight and its underlying displacement of the reactionary, enforced administration of political power in the period migrate subtly into Clare's encounter with his wealthy benefactor Admiral Lord Radstock. Radstock is initially full of praise for Clare's poetry with the condescending tone that only the truly powerful are capable of:

> ADMIRAL (*after nodding approval*) Your verse. Great charm there. True melody. Fine love of English landscape. (*Looks at* LAMB) Nothing mawkish – (*Turns back to* CLARE) a sailor or Christian may read it with profit. I'm both. When I was away with the fleet I often had such thoughts. Couldn't put them on paper though. (*F*, p. 124)

Radstock establishes the intrinsic literary merit of Clare's writing as expressing the quasi-moral values inherent in the English landscape. He then proceeds to advise Clare about those aspects of his work which require restraint – if not censorship. Radstock is concerned about what he views as a potentially dangerous radicalism in

Clare's implicit critique of the suffering rural poor. With patronising benevolence, Radstock mitigates this issue of socio-political protest as Clare's having 'The fault of a narrow horizon' (*F*, p. 124). Having made this concession for Clare's parochial short-sightedness, a coded judgement on his class and lack of formal education, he comes clearly and directly to the point:

> ADMIRAL I shan't lecture you. Political science isn't parish pump philosophy. But answer this. Who controls the brute in man? Polite society. Well, your verse undermines its authority. There'd be chaos. The poor would be the first to suffer. I understand some hangings have already been necessary in your part of the world. Makes my point for me. (*F*, p. 125)

The true nature and extent of the implementation of political power is made absolutely clear in 'some hangings have already been necessary'. When Mrs Emmerson supports the rationale of the Admiral shortly afterwards with, 'How does it help to shake your fist at heaven when some homeward-wending swain perishes in the snow?', Clare answers directly, 'They had a winter coat they 'ont perish' (*F*, p. 126).

The ultimate cost for Clare in daring to write of the real world through his poetry is disturbingly conveyed in the final, haunting scene in the asylum. Clare is pushed into the room in a wheelchair 'A shrivelled puppet. His head nods like a doll's.' The tragic irony of a writer now deprived of even the most basic language is overwhelming. It is not only Clare, the discarded literary novelty from the peasant class, who is incarcerated. Milton is also there, as is Napoleon who plays chess, reliving his great military victories. Milton's presence, along with Clare's, is the most tellingly cryptic about the wider social and economic forces that are sweeping away not only the poor but the former, land-based, quasi-feudal elite. Milton has become another emasculated, disposable commodity who has been disposed of his power and estate by his son. In this respect there is a subliminal sense of the perceived ingratitude and treachery of Fontanelle and Bodice:

> MILTON I can't sleep. See my wife's grave from the windows. Lie awake. Through the night. The dawn hurts my eyes. I hate my son.

A vicious bastard. I was cruel sometimes. Foolish. But did I hate? No. Never a hater [...] don't see much of him – except his back. Busy. In love with his factories. It's changed. D'you know who I am? (*F*, p. 151)

In the collection of poems published with the play entitled *Clare Poems*, the poem called 'Culture' contains the following verse:

> Reason is the mark of kin
> Poetry destroys illusions – it doesn't create them
> And hope is a passion that will not let men
> Rest in asylum's peace. (*F*, p. 155)

Michael Mangan makes the following most perceptive observation about the dramatic and thematic function of clusters of characters in *The Fool*:

> In Bond's plays there are frequently pairs of characters who function as aspects of each other (we have already seen Lear and his Ghost, Arthur and George) and Darkie is to some extent an aspect, or another version, of Clare himself – another casualty of an oppressive social system, who turns to violence rather than poetry and is destroyed because of it. Darkie also contains aspects of characters in other plays: for example, his rural activism connects him with the leveling activities of the puritan Son in *Bingo*, while he will reappear in another form as the Dark Man in *The Woman*. (1998, p. 36)

Restoration (1981)

In Peter Holland's article in the *Times Literary Supplement*, on 7 August 1981, about *Restoration* he makes a perceptive observation about its relationship to *The Fool*:

> In many ways, *Restoration* is closest in Bond's work to *The Fool* [...] It shares the same affectionate but unsentimentalised fascination with the East Anglian rural working class of the eighteenth century, the same horror at the identification of justice with the rights of the landowners, the same distress at the consequences of

the servants' humiliating subservience to that powerful hierarchy. (Qtd in Roberts, 1985, p. 48)

Reinelt perceptively observes of *Restoration*, Bond's 1981 political satire with songs:

> He configures [the character] Rose as black in order to allude through her to the knowledge of the history of slavery that informs her position in the play as the one most capable of understanding and resistance. (Reinelt, 1996, p. 52)

Bond himself develops this line of analysis in a letter he wrote to *The Guardian*, published on 31 July 1981:

> I looked around for what might be hopeful conflicts, conflicts that would perhaps rescue [Bob] from his fate. And I thought that in the racist conflict could be found a very good and informed political confrontation – a rational response to irrationality. (Qtd in Roberts, 1985, p. 49)

Restoration launched the decade of the 1980s for Bond. It was to be a difficult and traumatic one for him in terms of his presence in and relationship to the British theatre establishment. *Restoration* opened in a production at the Royal Court Theatre on 21 July 1981, directed by Bond. In his letter to *The Guardian* on 31 July 1981, Bond wrote: 'I was deeply depressed over the last [1979] election and, indeed, I wrote *Restoration* as a consequence. I saw [the protagonist] Bob as being the typical, working-class Tory voter, and the play is about his betrayal' (qtd in Roberts, 1985, p. 49). The election result of 1979 restored the Conservatives, the dominant party and political doctrine of twentieth-century British politics, to power. However, it was not simply the re-election of a right-wing political party. Through the largely unforeseen and ultimately meteoric rise to power of Margaret Thatcher, an aggressively new hybrid of anachronistic English nationalism was unleashed. This, in conjunction with a US-inspired monetarist economic policy and a commitment to dismantle the state and unleash free enterprise and privatisation, heralded a right-wing economic and social revolution that the Left could only have dreamt of achieving in equivalent socialist terms.

Meanwhile, in some of the most deprived areas of England's major cities, such as Toxteth in Liverpool and St Pauls in Bristol, areas of dense long-term unemployment, slum housing and established British ethnic communities, riots raged in the streets. As well as pre-figuring not only other major disturbances throughout the eighties caused by and in opposition to Thatcherite political policies, they prefigure the major riots in London and throughout the country in the summer of 2011.

Although Bond describes the setting for the play as 'England, eighteenth century – or another place at another time', *Restoration* depicts contemporary Britain in 1981, using the setting of eighteenth-century England as a critical mirror. In doing so, Bond exposes contemporary British society while distancing those events into a historical frame. The action of the play is interspersed with non-naturalistic songs to comment upon the principal themes and concerns.

A new song was added in some changes made to the original script after Thatcher's government embarked upon the Falklands War with Argentina in 1982. The South American country, ruled by a military junta at that time, sent forces to occupy and claim the disputed Falkland Islands in the South Atlantic, and the UK dispatched military forces in response. The Conservative administration was facing the prospect of a challenging contest at the forthcoming General Election and it was against this political backdrop that Thatcher and her advisors sensed that a military expedition would revive a collective reactionary revision and celebration of empire.

The ensuing war raged from 2 April to 14 June 1982 and there was inevitably a tragic loss of life on both sides. Many on the liberal-left were unhappy at the questionable premise on which war had been engaged by the British government. Perhaps the most enduring and iconic tragedy of the war which concluded with Argentina's surrender in June was the sinking by the British navy of the ARA *General Belgrano* warship on 2 May 1982; 323 Argentine lives were lost and over 700 rescued. The sinking of the *Belgrano* aroused powerful feelings and perspectives on both sides of the British political divide. The Rupert Murdoch-owned *Sun* celebrated the sinking with an infamous and ugly front-page headline in capital letters: 'GOTCHA!' Meanwhile, on the liberal-left, Tam Dalyell, a Labour MP, led a long-running campaign questioning the necessity and morality of the event. This focused especially but not exclusively on the fact that the ship had been outside the military exclusion zone when it was fired upon.

It was in the Royal Shakespeare's later, 1988 revival of the play that the song 'Legend of Good Fortune' was cut from scene 7 and replaced by the 'Falkland Song', sung by the Mother. The song eschews any simplistic morality, and questions with anger and tragic pathos the loss of all life in the conflict:

> MOTHER I don't know what the Spanish for suffering is
> Or the Spanish for mother or son or war
> Or the Spanish for winter or summer or pain
> Or for waste or for wounds or for wind or for rain
>
> My son it isn't for you that I mourn
> And I don't feel the pain of your flesh being torn
> I weep for the enemy you shot at Bluff Bay
> When the sun stood high on a cold winter day
> For the enemy you butchered on Tumbledown Height
> In the bayonet charge of the army of night
> But you don't hear what I say. (*R*, p. 283)

Bob, a young man from the East Anglian peasant class, arrives at the stately home of the socially aristocratic but financially bankrupt Lord Are. Bob's mother works as a housekeeper in Are's service and perfectly embodies the unthinking deference of the reactionary English working class to their ruling class. The compliant Bob has been framed by Are as the murderer of the aristocrat's wife, whom Are himself has callously and carelessly killed over breakfast. Their marriage had been predicated upon mutual economic advantage to her industrialist father, Hardache, and Are, whose sole concern now is to avoid the hangman's noose. Bob's mother sees her son's situation as a remarkable opportunity for social advancement:

> MOTHER [...] This is his big chance. Doo his lordship a favour like this an' he's set up for life. Poor people can't afford to waste a chance like this, god know it don't come often. Time our luck change [...] Ont expect his lordship to goo in the dock for the like of her. Jist drag his family name through the mire. Whatever

next! Ont know where to look next time I went to the village, they knew I work for someone like that. (*R*, pp. 237–8)

Prior to his arrest, Bob and his mother sought to detain for punishment one of their own servant class, Frank, for daring to steal some of the Are family silver. This was to subsidise his paltry wage and poor living conditions. Within the play, only Frank and Rose – Bob's young, black, Afro-Caribbean wife – offer any critique and resistance to the corrupt status quo. Rose also forcefully challenges Bob and his mother's internalised acceptance of the submission and oppression that it inflicts upon them. On realising that Bob is not the murderer – Are's wife, by Bob's admission, had blood on her before his arrival at the scene – Rose desperately seeks to raise the awareness of the other working-class characters. She commits herself to working for justice for Bob, who otherwise will face the death penalty. Exasperated and exhausted by her failure to make him understand his actual class position and fate, she asserts:

> ROSE You're a slave but you don't know it. My mother *saw* her chains, she's had marks on her wrists all her life. There are no signs on *you* till you're dead. How can yer fight for freedom when yer think you've got it? What happens to people like you? It's a circus! The clown kicks the mongrel and it licks his boots. He kicks it harder and it rolls on its back an' wags its tail – an' all the dogs laugh. Yer won't go. If there was a chance he'd put yer a mile underground an' chain yer to the wall. Then yer'd be free: yer'd know what you are. (*R*, p. 254)

The alliance between the aristocratic Are and the industrialist Hardache is an intrinsic and essential part of the treatment of the themes of the play and its historical counter-referencing. As Bond observed in 1981:

> The second half [of the play] concerns the creation of a new Lord Are – his alliance with Hardache was the basis for the English eighteenth century. His dementia in Scene 10 is the basis for modern fascism – which is a corruption of his alliance with Hardache. In other words, the play points at us from the eighteenth century and into the modern world. (Qtd in Roberts, 1985, p. 48)

By the final scene of the play, Bob has been executed, and the power and status of the English ruling class have been even more rooted and cemented by the 'new politics' of self-interest and expediency. This has been forged through Hardache's capital and the myth – constructed and sustained by Are and his class – of themselves as keepers of the sacred flames of nationhood, tradition and law-abiding godliness. In the final scene, Rose acknowledges: 'What have I learned? If nothing, then *I* was hanged' (*R*, p. 275). Determined not to be disempowered in an equivalent way to her dead husband, she exits with lines filled with the poignancy of loss but the commitment to return to the city and her part in the struggle for political change.

The four plays examined and discussed in this chapter all embody Bond's project in a period from 1971 to 1981 to revisit the past in order to engage in a radical excavation of the complex strata of English political and cultural history. This Goya-esque landscape whose interior he discovers, enters and explores is populated by men ruthlessly blinded by a totalitarian state. These men stagger into the hanging corpses of the poor, punished for their protests against the rich and powerful. Female revolutionaries run around them, ordering the execution of their reactionary enemies whilst screaming daughters howl at the doors of suicidal fathers and force them to face themselves in sharp mirrored shafts. Encircling this place is a wall like a straitjacket which builds, and builds, and builds.

I shall conclude this chapter with the following quote from Bond taken from a letter sent to Tony Coult on 28 July 1977. The date of this correspondence is significant in terms of the plays and related issues under discussion in this chapter. The first three plays in the quartet, *Lear*, *Bingo* and *The Fool*, had all been written and produced by this time. In this sense Bond's thoughts and sentiments expressed to Coult reflect where his thinking lay at that stage. Furthermore, written four years before the premiere of *Restoration*, the letter anticipates the more politically explicit plays which were to characterise Bond's writings in the 1980:

A rational, free culture is based on a classless society or at least on the conscious struggle to remove class structures [...] A writer's work should be part of this struggle. I've always felt that, but now I see more clearly what is involved. In *Bingo* I made Shakespeare lament that when he was old he no longer even understood the questions. We mustn't only write problem plays we must write answer plays [...] The answers aren't always light, easy or even straightforward, but the purpose – a socialist society – is clear. (Qtd in Roberts, 1985, p. 68)

The political, ideological certainty that was to inform the significant, landmark plays of the 1980s, ranging, after *Restoration*, through *Summer* (1982), *Derek* (1982), *Human Cannon* (1986) and *The War Plays* (trilogy, 1984–85), was to contrast significantly with the mood and perspective of Bond's plays from this point onwards, and especially so in the 'later plays'. It is in Bond's return to his earlier, ongoing questions and the posing of new ones in the 'later plays' that I will return to in Chapter 2, 'Learning to Sing in the Ruins'. As a prelude to that discussion, the edited transcript of my interview with Sean Holmes in November 2011, following on his critically acclaimed, successful revival of *Saved*, follows.

Interview 1
Staging *Saved*: Interview with Sean Holmes

This interview took place at the Lyric Theatre, Hammersmith, London in November 2011.

Peter Billingham (PB)   To begin with, Sean, I wanted to ask you what first attracted you to want to direct *Saved*, which is of course a classic play of the modern period.

Sean Holmes (SH)   Well, I think it was, if I'm honest, it was *the* play I most wanted to direct of any other plays. This was partly of course that it was a play that you hadn't been able to direct for a long period in England.

PB   That's right. When did you first encounter the play?

SH   I saw a production at the National Student Drama Festival when I was 17. Manchester University did a production of it. I just remember the shock of that play, being that age. I'm so glad I saw it at that age. Furthermore I can't remember the stoning scene interestingly. And I remember the shock of that play, that shock of that subject for me at that age. I remember the 'stockings' scene [scene 9] the 'fishing' scene [scene 6]. I'm very clear in my memory of that scene. I was very into drama, I studied my Drama A levels and was really taken by drama. We were studying [Bond's] *Lear* at A level and so I was aware of Edward Bond and I was kind of blown away by the power of that play as well. Seeing it, it made so much more sense for me. It was a play I always wanted to do. I was lucky enough to direct *The Sea* about ten years ago at The Minerva Studio at The Chichester Festival Theatre and so I got to know Edward through that.

PB   What are your memories of that production at Chichester?

SH   Edward liked *The Sea*. He wasn't around as much in rehearsals as much as he was subsequently later for *Saved*. However, he tried to be around and he saw a performance of the play. After that, we had correspondence and at various times over the next ten years from various theatres I tried to get the performing rights to *Saved*. During that period, like lots of other directors, I failed.

PB   Was that so? What then happened?

SH   I think he might remember this differently. I think he did say, 'If I was going to let anyone do it, I'd let you, Sean. But I'm not going to let you do it' [*Smiles*].

PB   What happened subsequently?

SH   We were lucky enough to just be where we are now. So over a year ago now, I had a chat with Tom [Edward Bond's agent] about something else. At the end of our phone conversation, I said, are you actually going to let me do *Saved*? Tom said that was a great idea! Of course, I thought, oh, I'll believe that when I see it but we did! Obviously, it was the start of a bigger conversation with Edward about not just doing *Saved* in isolation but doing it with 'The Chair Plays' [the trilogy of *Have I None, The Under Room* and *Chair*]. I think it's very important that *Saved* is then being framed by the later works. To me that seemed essential.

PB   That's one of the things that I'm going to be looking at in my research. It's the way in which seeds of themes and concerns that were planted in an early classic like *Saved* continued to develop through the 'later plays'.

SH   Yes, that's right.

PB   Those seeds grew and through into those plays that I call the 'later plays', from 1995 and 2000 onwards.

SH   Yes, I see.

PB   Interestingly not much has been written and published on those 'later plays'.

SH   I see.

PB   What strikes me through my own reading and research is just how deep and consistent Edward's principal concerns remain.

SH   I agree.

PB   Once you began work on *Saved* what was the biggest challenge that you discovered for yourself as the director?

SH   I think there are several things. One is a kind of aesthetic yet also a very practical problem. For me, it's a very simple challenge. It's sort of a 'design' challenge although it's bigger than that. It's about the world in which you set the play. Edward said to me, anyone who sets the play in 1965 would be mad. This was a very useful and important point to consider. My instinct was very much with Edward in this and I said to the actors on the first day of rehearsal that the least interesting thing about the play is its period. It's the thing that is of the least interest. What I felt very strongly was that if we wrapped it in a period, then it would soften its impact. Because you could watch it and say, 'oh, that was happening *then*'.

PB   Yes, that's right.

SH   It was different with a play like *Chicken Soup with Barley* [by Arnold Wesker] in the production at the Royal Court because there the period obviously needs to be clear. In that play the dramatic action actually travels over several decades and you need a clear timeline conveyed.

PB   I agree.

SH   That was very useful in my thinking. They will know if we create the world of *Saved* on stage as if it were locked in the past, then we're not really 'releasing' the play. I know this must seem obvious but, you know, there is the world *of* the play. It's the world of that play that you set it in. Does that make sense? That's what I think what we did with the design and the setting and it must have worked because nobody really noticed it. The set was quite abstract. It was, to use Edward's phrase, 'the site' in which the event could happen. The clothes, whilst being reminiscent of the sixties, are almost all from the present day.

PB   Sure.

SH   And the props, interestingly, all ended up being mostly from the eighties. They looked old but they weren't 'singing out' 'We're from the sixties!' It was very tricky because we're so used to being able to read the cut of the jacket, the style of a pair of shoes or even a hair-cut. These things say something powerfully about period and class.

PB   Yes, of course, fashion itself is a form of cultural commodity.

SH   I think that was very important in the production because then it's very much what Edward is about, in a way. That is, presenting human behaviour with no obstacles or distractions in the way – very purely and simply, so that the 'metaphor of performance' could be read into it by the audience as well. It seems to me that that's the other thing that's very important. That was the first challenge. When you sit there thinking about the play it's how you preserve that sense of authenticity. It's one of the things I felt we mostly got right. The second challenge though was in terms of casting. It's such a brilliant play and I felt that I met with lots of younger actors who I really admire and liked and liked to work with. But I realised quite quickly that it wasn't right because they were, maybe, a few years too old. They're sort of middle twenties. There was a sort of life-experience, a particularity, that wasn't quite right. So, we ended up really with – apart from the actors playing Harry and Mary – a very young, rela-tively inexperienced cast. This was very important, I think, to the success of those performances. There was a sort of genuineness, a lack of artifice and a kind of openness to the writing that really gave it a lot. Again I think it gave an extra contemporary feeling, because there is in all these things something which is very modern, very 'London', speaking the language in 1965. That again seemed to fit in between the two worlds of the past and the present. I think the third challenge I faced was obviously that it's a very complex play.

PB   It's very layered in all kinds of ways.

SH   I think there's something about it that's especially interesting. For a complex play, it's not nevertheless dense. It's deep, deep of course. You can actually put the scene together on some kind of level, quite easily. It's not like doing other plays which are very impenetrable. It's about what's going on underneath and underneath and underneath. In that important sense rehearsal became very much like a kind of archaeology where we'd dig a layer there, skilfully and carefully and with great attention to detail. The other thing is that Edward, more than any other writer I've ever directed a play by, writes so completely in three dimensions that the image is so strong as to what's happening on stage. For example, the way that he gave importance to the chair or a teacup or a box of matches: a pram.

PB Yes, there's a tremendous sense of detail and he's often talked about how drama must embrace the edge of the table and also the edge of the universe.

SH Yes and he understands the way that it becomes classical Greek drama in a South London council house. You know it's rather extraordinary. And you have to find *both* things.

PB One of the things that I really liked about the production was that it had a strong sense of 'epic scale' yet also had a directness and lack of 'clutter' in the way it communicated with its audience.

SH Yes, thank you.

PB It had a kind of grandeur, you could say, a classic quality but also the absolute, particular detail of the here and the now. One of the things I really liked about the production was the sense of the actors being tremendously direct and open and – in that sense – courageous.

SH I think that's right. It was a really interesting journey for all of us, you know, to find how you live in that world and also discovering how the play changes as well, particularly after the death of the baby. The play seems in the second half that it's becoming much more abstract. As Edward also said to us, it's as if the dead baby is present in some way in every scene.

That sense of the presence of the baby in every scene requires one to think about how one makes that journey and how one keeps it in that place and at a proper pace. For example, I remember with the 'stocking scene'. You know of course the first time you do it, you do what you've done in the rehearsal room. You do what you do in rehearsal, and the audience is having hysterics. The second or third performance was that, you can't help it, you pick up on the laughs. Then you realise how wrong that is and so you have to find a way to play that scene and that moment with absolute seriousness. It's an awful scene of 'abuse' in which Mary exploits and pressurises Len.

PB Yes, that's right.

SH One of the things which I think was great is how, in rehearsal, Edward would use a question to unleash the actors' imagination.

This was in order for the *actors* to find the answer. You can't be expected for that always to happen in the creative process because we don't have that long rehearsals. You get used to the actors expecting to be given 'answers' by the director. As much as you try to work in a democratic way, as I hope I would, often time pressures mean you can't. You think if I could help an actor, then, that could save me that couple of hours that I haven't got otherwise. It's that thing about holding on till we – not get it right – because you have to get it right, but trying to create the space where real discoveries and decisions can be made.

PB   That must be so important.

SH   Yes, that's right – it is.

PB   I first saw *Saved* in 1972 when I was a young drama student. It was just beginning to be produced after the original ban. I remember that it was the final scene that stayed in my memory. When I saw it in your production, I thought in a way that I hadn't before that there was a presence of Ionesco.

SH   Yes, in the final scene?

PB   I'd always thought that this play and its final scene is not social realism. Understandably perhaps the critics of the original production did talk about the play in precisely those terms.

SH   I've done quite a lot of those plays that are much closer to social realism, but have that poetry about them like David Storey's work.

PB   Yes, that's right.

SH   Of course because it was set where it was set in terms of its location and characters, it would have been seen as social realism to some degree because of the period it was set in. Increasingly you know, however, it seems to me very obvious that actually *Saved* is about being human. It's not actually about particular concerns or the particularities of society in 1965. It's about how we live in society. Also as with all great writers – and Edward emailed me yesterday saying something like this – what happens is that all great writers *predict*. It's almost like it can't happen until they've written it. I felt this very strongly when I was doing *Blasted* by Sarah Kane. It was very interesting because, of course, when we did it, the play's relevance had become more obvious. What Edward was observing in *Saved* was that something destructive was happening in society and that it could get worse. Now we're in a place where from the beginnings of consumerism in the early sixties, it's grown to dominate the world.

PB   We're strangled by it.

SH   Yes, that's right.

PB   What, in the beginning would have been viewed with a kind of optimism, the possibility of a better standard of living. I mean, I grew up in a traditional working-class family. People like my dad and mum had to work very hard, and there was nothing extra. To them, who had grown up effectively in poverty, it must have looked like what we see as consumerism might work out well for them.

SH   Yes, of course.

PB   I think that Edward would never want to be thought of as 'prophetic' in any literal sense. I think, however, that his is a kind of voice that comes in from the edge, the one that speaks into society from the outside –

SH   Yes, absolutely.

PB   – With a dramatic and political vision that he can't and won't compromise. Neither should he of course.

SH   Yes. That's very good, I agree. It's interesting, of course, that that's in the play in a funny way. Len is a kind of 'alien' in the world of the play. You know, Len is an 'outsider'. Len asks questions. Len talks. Len tries to change things. Len tries to save Pam, which she doesn't want to be.

PB   Yes.

SH   It's very complicated.

PB   I'm working on *The Children* at the moment with an undergraduate cast. I was in rehearsal with them yesterday. They were talking about the Stranger, the character who is killed in the fire that is started by Joe 'under order' from his mother. The cast asked whether the Stranger could be there witnessing the rest of the events 'posthumously' throughout the play. In *Saved*, of course, Len witnesses the stoning to death of the baby, yet does not participate in it or intervene to try and stop it. It's possible perhaps to see the role of the dramatist through the character and perspective of Len in *Saved*. Here is someone of a specific environment and site, of a class, both *in* the world of that play and yet, somehow, at its margins? I thought the young actor who played Len was very 'real'. In that realism there was a kind of vulnerability which I really recognised and admired.

SH   Thank you. That's right. I really think the difference between reading the play and hearing it read is of course, when you read it, things are concrete and of a certain tone throughout.

PB   Yes, of course.

SH   But, of course, it's so rich and varied and layered.

PB   Yes, the radical subtext beneath the surface.

SH   For the actor that was an interesting journey to find that out and in fact explore with that language because the language you get – and this refers back to your previous point, Peter – the language is not 'naturalistic'.

PB   That's right; it's more layered and muscular in terms of its dramatic impact.

SH   It was undoubtedly an important journey for that actor.

PB   I wonder if that was one of the challenges that so many of the critics of the 1965 production faced. Apart from the devastating shock of scene 6, of course, was the main challenge: 'Where do we *place* this play? What kind of vocabulary have we got to engage with and discuss it? What is its *site*?'

SH   Yes, I agree.

PB   You can understand in that context why critics and audiences thought, well, it *must* be social realism.

SH   Yes.

PB   You've got this young writer. *Saved* is his first major play with a public audience, because of course *The Pope's Wedding* had been a Sunday evening only 'production without décor'. *Saved* was therefore a kind of explosion in a public space.

SH   That's absolutely right. It's like one of the best well-made plays. It's perfectly formed. The world of the play in one sense is familiar and recognisable. Yet, it's so strange, you don't expect it. It's about people ironing, or people eating their dinners or watching television or sitting in the café or mending a chair. All of those things are given an incredible weight and moment and significance. These contrasts are very difficult to talk about and how those things in the play disturb, engage and provoke us, you know?

PB   Of course when Edward Bond wrote an introduction to the published version of the play, he talked about *Saved* being 'irrepressibly optimistic'.

SH   Yes, that's right.

PB   I was wondering whether you think that it's less possible now to talk of optimism relating to the play, given the social and political conditions in our contemporary world.

SH   What is interesting is that in the last scene of the play you don't know if he repairs the chair. Does he try any more? He seems to yet it still wobbles. He tries it again, and it wobbles. He leans on it and he twists it, which is probably the best solution. Instead he leans on the chair in that strange, sort of 'Michelangelo' posture at the end.

PB   Yes.

SH   I think this play is suspended between optimism and despair. I think elsewhere Edward mentions that if he kicks the chair, that would be optimistic.

PB   I hadn't come across that, it's interesting.

SH   It's the humanness of what you think can – or might – be possible. The more we hope, the more we think, the more we want to achieve it. I do wonder within that moment: is it fixed?

PB   I wonder. I don't think it can or *should* be.

SH   If it's fixed, it just confirms what the play's been telling us.

PB   There's an ancient Jewish story. It's about persistence to achieve positive change and the necessity of human action in order for the change to happen. The story says that if you're planting an orchard or even planting one single tree towards an orchard and you think you see a Messiah is coming, don't stop working: keep planting the tree. Progressive change of any meaningful, sustained kind is 'in our hands' alone.

SH   Yes.

PB   I just thought what a simple but profound and wonderful story. The pragmatism and 'hope' involved in planting a tree. A belief in the present providing the possibility for a future. Always take and trust the action in the here and now. Len trusts the action of the here and now – regardless.

SH   It's great.

PB   It's the action that makes a difference, because without action, it remains an ideal, an abstraction. I guess that, inevitably, when I think of that final scene where there's no obvious basis for optimism in the present or the future.

SH   Yes, yes.

PB   There remains the possibility of change. Len continues to 'plant a tree' without any external incentive. I don't mean by that some form of simplistic 'positivism'.

SH   The thing is it also comes towards the end of the previous scene, the penultimate scene. There, Harry tries to get Len to stay. Len finds out that Harry's reasons are mad – basically dreams. 'I killed a man.' You'd think these things would make Len leave but instead he stays but not because of Harry. Or rather, something to do with the scene with Harry is that Harry's motivation is revenge.

PB   Yes.

SH   Someone has to 'pay' for the past although you're not sure that they will. The other really interesting thing about this play is silence. Actually the play is built on silence. The dominant mode of communication in the play is not talking but silence.

PB   Yes, I see.

SH   Talk in itself means something and often it's Len who unleashes it. If you took Len out of a lot of those scenes, would there be a conversation?

PB   We've talked about the challenges of working on the play and the unique characteristics and demands of Bond's writing.

SH   That's right.

PB   I wonder whether you could identify any other moments in that journey with your cast that are worth sharing.

SH   I think there are different things. In any show actors have their crucial challenges, their defining moments, you know? They struggle. One of the really difficult scenes was the 'teapot' scene. It's interesting – Edward said he wasn't quite a good enough writer at the time to really write what he wanted in the scene. He knew what's going on and what's not going on in the scene, but not quite in control of how it reveals itself.

PB   Yes, I see.

SH   I mean there are the dynamics going on between the four of them and it's a difficult scene because of that. It was interesting what Edward said on one occasion. There was one rehearsal when he was very 'interventionist'. Actually not so much interventionist but challenging us more than he had done up until then.

PB   Could you say a little more?

SH   He said, I'm really sorry about this but it's how I am. He also said, it's because, actually, the scene [with the teapot incident] is better than it's ever been but it can still be much, much better. Actually, it was the right provocation. It's a very difficult balance. I think it was something that was sometimes difficult for the actors.

PB   Yes.

SH   Sometimes, you have to acknowledge that the actors aren't quite getting there in a particular scene but that's alright. You know, we know, it *isn't* but then we'll come back later in rehearsals to make it alright.

PB   Yes, I see.

SH   So that was the challenge with the rhythms of that scene. I think, ultimately, Edward's challenge was right and it did make the scene – and the play – better. Pam is a deeply unsympathetic character – and

I think Lea who played her did an extraordinary job. She shouts and screams but you have to find a bit of fragility and vulnerability there. Because of course she loves Fred like Len loves her. The problem is the madness of these different and conflicting loves. Mary and Harry's relationship is built in some weird way on lust or some sort of attraction. You wouldn't feel the moment they speak that within two pages one of them would smash the other over the head with a teapot! That wouldn't exist without some kind of passion, however strange or odd between them. There's a lot of 'heat' in the play, weirdly.

PB Yes, emotional and psychological intensity, although it's as much located in the dramatic site as it is in individual characters.

SH The stoning is a challenging scene. It's very demanding and it was very useful to have Edward there. What you realise is that there are so many key dramatic moments in that scene. There is not a mob rush to violence and nobody wants to kill the baby to start with – they want to go out for the night – there are '510 moments' where the baby might not die. It's about what's going on in that moment. Then somebody does something, he messes someone's suit up, someone else says something that winds someone up, you're in one specific moment after another but they're all connected. I think it's being really in control of all of that because, as I say, each moment builds, one moment leads to the other, to the other, to the other. To get to that, again, to go beyond the mob, to get the actors to go deep into their characters and explore their own particularity is crucial. I think that's why I was so pleased with that scene and with the actors in that scene. When you think about scene 6 what you remember are five, really clear individuals doing things for slightly different reasons even if you don't know what the reasons were. To me, that's the thing that I love best in theatre, the thing that I'm most engaged with as an audience member from a young age. I wasn't really able to articulate it. It's when you see something that you actually believe that it's true and real but you don't understand. You can't easily understand. And your mouth drops open. The truth of that moment hits you before your brain can rationalise why it's happened.

I think that *Saved* is an obvious example of a play that does that so often. You could see that in the reaction of the audience. Actually we're lucky in this theatre to have a younger, more diverse audience. I remember the very first preview when I looked around and, basically, everyone was under 25 and mostly in school or college groups. The first half was an hour and a half. Oh well I thought 'we've had it' with such a young audience as that generation allegedly has such a low attention span.

PB   Allegedly, yes.

SH   Of course, it was the polar opposite, because people have an attention span if something is worth paying attention to. What was so interesting with that audience was the absolute connection which that generation had with that play.

PB   I was at the final preview and certainly, on that evening, you could hear a pin drop. That young audience was really attentive.

SH   I know – it was amazing.

PB   In scene 6, the silence was resounding.

SH   I think that's the interesting thing. That's why the play is that sort of play. The play trades in silence itself but the silence is also placed on the audience itself. I know I've never quite heard that in any other play I've done.

PB   It's remarkable.

SH   There was a moment, a real moment, you know in the final scene. The stage direction says 'Stop'. And then you think, what has stopped? It's the moment they all look up. What you could feel in the audience in this already silent scene was that you could feel the silence 'thicken'. It was just that. I've never experienced that in the theatre before. This strange, thick silence – communal.

PB   It reminds me of when I went to see *The Gladiator Games* by Tanika Gupta – the transcript Verbatim Theatre piece – at the Theatre Royal, Stratford East.

SH   Yes.

PB   I'd never been in an auditorium where there were so many young people. I was very different by age, ethnicity and race from just about everyone else there. It was in the scene where the white racist talks about having murdered this young Asian detainee with whom he shares a prison cell. There was this groundswell of noise, like a large wave breaking on a shingle beach: a collective, communal intake of breath.

SH   Amazing.

PB   To the point where I thought that someone was going to run up onto the stage and assault or at least challenge the actor playing the part of the racist. It was tremendous to be there and to experience that. However, in a sense the power of what *Saved* was doing to its young audience was on an even deeper level.

SH   Of course, *Saved* is dealing with what it means to be human on the deepest and most profound level. This is not to denigrate that other show of course.

PB   No, of course not. It was a strong piece of its kind. I'm not a 'fan' of Verbatim Theatre as a genre.

SH   Just to say that there's something deeper within *Saved* because it hits you in ways you can't understand. You know, you can't say, I felt this because of that. Also it provokes. The other thing, of course, is that if you speak to a hundred different people and say that, you provoke a hundred different reactions. In terms of that final scene, in terms of the reaction to the stoning or other moments in the play, there are many possible reactions.

PB   Interestingly, I'd been giving a lecture on *Saved* to first-year Drama students [at the University of Winchester] earlier this week. A student asked me, 'Why was there only that one line of dialogue in the final scene of the play?' That's Len's 'Fetch me 'ammer.'

SH   That's right.

PB   I said, I wouldn't presume to give the student 'the answer' so to speak but I'd gladly share with her my own thoughts. I said that the absence of language speaks volumes about the relationship between these characters and their environment. By the end of the play, despite everything that has happened, they are still in this silence. I asked the student, 'Who does Bond give the one line of dialogue to? What line does he give him? What might it mean, especially in a symbolic sense?'

SH   Of course.

PB   It's strange, really. We talk about living in a very visual culture, for young people, especially, and of course they do. Actually however language is also very important to them.

SH   That's absolutely right.

PB   It's going to be interesting working on the other three plays in the season in April and May next year. Will you be working with any of the same cast?

SH   We'd really like to – there's not such a clear correlation – really most of the characters are probably a bit younger than Harry and Mary and a bit older than the bulk of the young people.

PB   I can see that, yes.

SH   It would be lovely, I mean, I think it would be very, very useful to have actors who've done *Saved* because you have that, sort of 'Bond in your bones'.

PB   Yes.

SH   This is very useful.

PB   Of course.

SH   It would save a lot of time so that's something we'd have to look at.

PB   Had you ever thought that you might try and run the season as a season in itself with the trilogy following on from – or preceding – *Saved*?

SH   We did but one major issue was that there was a practical problem about having to be rehearsing the plays around the same time. So, that was initially our thought. This however became an even better way of doing it, I think.

PB   I like the idea, actually, of the trilogy almost being a kind of echo in response to *Saved*.

SH   Yes, that's right.

PB   You drop a stone in the water, so to speak, in the autumn, and then in the spring the ripples continue to move and resonate?

SH   Yes, I agree, I think it will be very interesting to do that. What's also interesting is that in the intervening period the Young Vic will be doing *Bingo* as well, the one they're bringing in from Chichester. So, that will be on as well in between *Saved* and 'The Chair Plays' trilogy.

PB   I'm delighted of course that there is this revival of interest in Edward Bond's plays at this time.

SH   Yes, it's wonderful, I agree.

PB   I suppose it began with Jonathan Kent's revival of *Lear* at the Sheffield Crucible Theatre about five or six years ago?

SH   Yes, that's right –

PB   Then Rupert Goold's revival of *Restoration*.

SH   *Restoration*, yes, that's right, in about 2006.

PB   With Jonathan Kent then directing *The Sea* at the Haymarket, which was remarkably Edward Bond's first appearance in the West End.

SH   Is that so?

PB   Why is there this resurgence of interest in British theatre in this period do you think? Of course, since 1995 he's been writing continuously for Big Brum and is also very successful in France, especially Paris in the same period.

SH   Well, because, I mean: is there a better writer alive at the present? Those plays are really important. Those plays contain things that very few plays nowadays do. The thing for me was the privilege of spending that time with Edward was his deep, consistent, constant searching thoughts about theatre.

PB   I know exactly what you mean.

SH   It was profound and you don't have those conversations very often in theatre and that is crucial for me. That's what I mean about it being quite transformative for me. There is this idea that Edward Bond is really difficult to work with and have in the rehearsal room from some quarters. In my experience, that's completely wrong. We experienced the complete opposite and we were able to form a relationship which was a proper one between a director and writer. I found the production was much better as a result because why wouldn't you want that? He wasn't didactic, he wasn't controlling. He was provoking in the right way. The thing is that it is his imagination and his way of looking at the world. It's so particular and so stimulating that it can only help inform everyone in that room.

PB   It must have felt a real privilege?

SH   For everyone, it was. It was that sense that he had been in exile and that he really, really worked so hard for those six or seven weeks. We were very lucky we did a workshop with a group of younger writers: good writers, but sort of 'Royal Court Upstairs'. It was meant to be 'How do you begin to write for bigger spaces?' but it was in fact 'How'd you write the best possible play?' I think they all found it brilliantly stimulating.

PB   What a great opportunity for them.

SH   He even wrote very graciously to them after the event, at the end of the workshop. He was very challenging and provocative in the best possible sense. The trouble is we just don't usually have those kinds of conversations that you end up having with Edward. Whatever else it is that we're doing, we're also hopefully doing something some of the time that is quite profound and ancient: making art.

PB   I do think that the criticisms of Edward Bond and his work that took root in some areas of British theatre over the years are a depressing reflection of a wider cultural and political malaise.

SH   The thing is he's uncompromising. He actually feels he's compromised too much in a theatre world where so much is based on compromise: often to its detriment. I think there's a problem not only with theatre culture but the wider culture that we all live in. I'm really aware that as somebody running a theatre and trying to keep 40 people and yourself in a job, and of my responsibility with the tax-payers' money that funds us and all of those things.

PB   Yes, of course.

SH   Not to have an empty theatre but also to try and be challenging. I think that's what's been fantastic about doing *Saved* is I'm too
young to have seen *Saved* being done professionally in my lifetime
prior to now.

PB   Yes.

SH   So there are an awful lot of people who know the play and
are aware of the play, but have never seen it. I think it will have an
impact in all sorts of ways on theatre. On writers and performers,
everyone. It had an obvious impact at the time in terms of the ultimate abolition of stage censorship. What's 'shocking' now I think
is the form, is the craft and extraordinariness of what he's doing in
that play.

PB   There is a strong sense that the political as well as the dramatic
concerns that he is writing about from *The Hidden Plot* [2000] onwards
and in what I call the 'later plays' are present and evident in an early
play like *Saved*. The mix of the social, political and existential – Bond
would also say, ontological – that distinguishes him especially from
other modern and contemporary British playwrights?

SH   To me, it's the closest thing you're ever going to get to working
with Shakespeare.

PB   Yes, absolutely – or possibly our contemporary Euripides?

SH   Edward Bond ultimately along with all of the best writers understands how extraordinarily strange we all are. That's why bad writing
is so bad because it just shows you all the clichés about how people
supposedly are.

PB   That's right.

SH   Bond is always writing in three dimensions. It's always the
image he's seeing. As you direct it, you start to see what he sees. You
know, you can see the power of the visual dimension of theatre.

PB   I know exactly what you mean.

SH   I remember working on *The Sea* very clearly as a young director
and you have that wonderful scene on the cliff tops. You have the

piano and the cremated ashes suddenly flying everywhere! This kind of layered, three-dimensional dramatic vision is the most extraordinary thing I'd ever come across.

It's an amazing thing. It's extraordinary. And again, how deeply profound that is and in ways you can't always understand. He's presenting you with the contradictions and having the audience read what they will from it.

PB   It's interesting. I wonder if you know the story. Edward has talked about how the first time that he saw a play in performance was Donald Wolfit in and as *Macbeth* whilst he was still at school [see e.g. Roberts, 1985, p. 7]. He talked about how for the first time he saw something on stage which reflected and recognised the world he lived in. I think that world of violence must have reflected his own experience of growing up as a young child in the Second World War and the trauma of evacuation. Later, after the war, his experience of national service was also profoundly unsettling and traumatic. It's hard not to see that exerting a very powerful influence upon his emerging and later thinking.

SH   I didn't know that but I can see that's right.

PB   Sean, I wonder if I can ask just one final question?

SH   Sure.

PB   What's your 'barometer reading' of both British theatre and its relationship to our contemporary society which is facing so many critical challenges and threats?

SH   I think what is difficult is that the prevailing culture – the media, even political – is so monoculture. It's very hard for theatre to get out from under that. The pressures are on it in terms of how you sell the shows, especially in London where there is so much work being produced. I worked at the Donmar. It was one of the happiest experiences I've had – a brilliant time – and I was very proud of the show. But if you look at the Donmar, it's *a* model of success not *the* model of success. Not the only model of success. It seems to me though in the wider field of contemporary theatre that there is an absence of a kind of oppositional theatre or thinking of different ways about going about making theatre. I think that this has led to a small 'c' conservatism in terms of what is produced. Actors have to look at themselves and of course directors and writers as well. Directors, obviously: are we being as brave or as experimental or as honest as we should be? You know, everything I'm saying applies to me as much as anyone else. I feel working with Edward Bond on *Saved* has shown that there are directions that we should be travelling in more often.

PB   Thanks, Sean.

SH   Thanks, Peter.

2
Learning to Sing in the Ruins: The Later Plays, 1999–2011

In this chapter I shall be discussing seven defining plays from Bond's later and most recent works. These plays all date from the period that I refer to as the 'later plays'. They are, in terms of chronological order: *The Crime of the Twenty-First Century* (1999). *The Children* (2000), *Have I None* (2000), *Chair* (2000), *The Under Room* (2005), *Tune* (2007) and *Innocence* (published 2011). My aim is to explore the extent to which these recent and contemporary works reflect and embody ongoing thematic and dramatic concerns from across Bond's entire output. Simultaneously I analyse the extent to which plays from this period signal the emergence of a new and distinctive stage and vision in Bond's dramatic intentions, aims and craft. These plays, as explained in the Introduction, fall under, and to some extent cross, two defining generic headings for Bond's work as a whole. They are 'The Paris Plays' and 'The Birmingham Plays'. These two series have arguably provided Bond with a context in which to work with more freedom and opportunity as a playwright in the light of what seems to be his continuing exploration and experimentation with dramatic form, structure and purpose. In his Introduction, entitled 'The Third Crisis', to *The Chair Plays* he observes:

> We shall not know ourselves until we can create these future fictions to be responsible for our own present lives, not know ourselves till we know them and not know how to live till they teach us. Perhaps that is how we will restore the profundity and scope that made drama the basis of modern civilization. (Bond, 2012a, p. xxi)

These 'future fictions' that Bond refers to he has identified earlier in the Introduction in this way:

> If human beings no longer belong in the world there will still be some sort of beings that survive us. We are preparing the catastrophe they will live in. They will not remember our world. They will know the sterile despair of their own world and have no hope. They will be the creatures we have created and their symptoms will be worse than ours. For that reason they should be the subject of our plays. But there is a more profound reason, one closer to the logic of drama. Because if to be human means to know your world and your situation in it absolutely, then they will be more human than we are. (2012a, p. xxi)

It is arguable and possible I believe to view the 'later plays' from this perspective that Bond himself presents. The plays might be viewed therefore as presenting us as contemporary audiences as 'future fictions' of ourselves. Crucially these fictions might also be open to interpretation as signifiers of our contemporary crisis, whilst, paradoxically, subtly suggesting what might evolve as the human.

Some of these plays, including *At the Inland Sea* and *Have I None*, were commissioned and written specifically for young audiences. They constitute 'The Birmingham Plays'. However, a number of them have subsequently had productions in other theatres and to adult audiences in both Paris and London and elsewhere. For this reason and for the purposes of this chapter I have decided to structure my discussion of the 'later plays' in the following way. I shall discuss under the subheading of 'The Paris Plays' two of the original plays in that series, *The Crime of the Twenty-First Century* and *Innocence*. In addition under that heading I shall also be discussing *Have I None* as it enjoyed its non-English premiere in Paris in 2003. Then under the subheading of 'The Birmingham Plays' I shall discuss *Chair, The Under Room* and *Tune*. In addition I shall be discussing *The Children*, which I directed with an undergraduate student cast from the University of Winchester in 2012. The first production of *The Children* was presented by Classworks Theatre on 11 February 2000 at Manor Community College, Cambridge. The play was commissioned as part of a wider project to explore critical social and ethical issues relating to young people from disadvantaged backgrounds.

Have I None was one of many plays originally commissioned by Big Brum Theatre in Education company and directed by Chris Cooper. In discussing them I shall be placing them in the context of Bond's wider and ongoing commitment to write for young people. I shall explore and refer to the revival (April 2012) of *Have I None* as part of the exciting season of Bond's plays under the heading of 'The Chair Plays' produced by Sean Holmes at the Lyric Theatre, Hammersmith, London in the autumn of 2011 and spring 2012.

There are some potentially interesting thematic correlations and dramatic echoes between a major early play such as *Saved* and 'later plays' such as *Chair* and *Have I None*. The chair is of course an important if not as controversially iconic dramatic object and metaphor as the pram in *Saved*. Both the chair and the pram have a primary and customary domesticated function within and with allusions to the home, family and childhood. Len memorably and significantly seeks to repair the broken chair in the last scene of *Saved*. The chair has been broken by a fight between Harry and his existentially estranged wife Mary. The fight has been provoked over Harry's knowledge of the potentially intimate relationship between his wife and Len. As Mangan helpfully observes:

> The final scene of the play shows the family sitting down quietly and getting on with their everyday lives as Len (who had been about to leave the house, but eventually decided to stay) mends the broken chair. It is because of this simple gesture that Bond described the play at the time as being 'almost irresponsibly optimistic'. (Mangan, 1998, p. 16)

However, this provisional optimism with which *Saved* ends is powerfully contrasted with the metonymic meaning of the chair in the play of that title. It has a darkly, arguably tragic functional use as the means by which Alice commits suicide. It is open to interpretation that this action also carries potential connotations as a liberating theatre event through which Billy will be impelled to enter out into the dangerous world beyond the relatively safe haven of their shared home. The oblique hope in the ending of *Saved* written in a period of cautious social and political optimism contrasts powerfully with Billy's ultimate death in an alien and violent urban world where optimism has vaporised – even as have Alice's ashes.

It is against this backdrop that I shall now turn in my discussion to an examination of *The Crime of the Twenty-First Century*.

'The Paris Plays'

The Crime of the Twenty-First Century (1999)

After a May 1999 German premiere, *The Crime of the Twenty-First Century* was produced on 9 January 2001 at the Théâtre national de la Colline, Paris, and was directed by Alain Françon. On the title page of the 2003 Methuen edition of this play, Bond has placed the infamous quotation from Thatcher, 'there is no such thing as society'. This statement both epitomises the core ideological values of the Thatcher period and provides a parallel for a dramatic site in which Bond envisions the implications of a brutally autocratic, postmodern state. The setting of the piece is, to quote from Bond's stage directions, 'an open space that was once a yard or two or three ground-floor rooms. It is in the "clearance," a vast desert of ruins that stretch for hundreds of miles and has been flattened to discourage resettlement.' This landscape of material devastation and decay might be analogous to post-atomic Hiroshima, Belsen or the war-ravaged, occupied territory of Palestine or Iraq. However, this dramatic site is more powerfully and significantly a scenic political metaphor rather than literal. Four characters inhabit this bleak landscape: two men, Grig and Sweden, and two women, Hoxton and Grace, mother and daughter. These characters speak in a savagely clipped, idiomatic, post-holocaust dialect:

> GRIG Let the effect a' the water wear off. Why's the road so straight? Army made it when they flat all this. White makes yer eyes run. Left me place – no permit. Wife was dyin. Scream – yer could count the interval, regular as a siren [...] Death takes its time to tell its tale: 'ers was cancer. When it reached 'er mouth she scream as if it's arguing with 'er in 'er throat. (*CTFC*, p. 7)

Reduced to the most elemental scavenging for water, food and shelter, these characters engage in fearful bartering and sharing of the most basic ingredients for survival. Beyond these brutally marginalised 'clearances' (redolent of ethnic cleansing in the Bosnian War in the former Yugoslavia), the characters speak of a wider world of prisons and punishment camps. There are also oppressive suburbs and ghettos where an undefined privileged class continues to enjoy the residual benefits of consumer capitalism, particularly cars. It is a world bereft of any social organisation other than an army that continually patrols the clearances. These forces dismember and blind those from the marginalised underclass, such as Sweden; only the desperately fundamental instinct for survival holds sway. Yet, under such extreme conditions, Bond creates characters who, though stripped of all socially and culturally conditioned attitudes, still seek some fundamental form of social interaction. Hoxton gives water, and subsequently shelter, to Grig when he arrives at her minimal lodging. At the conclusion of the play, when Sweden has murdered both Hoxton and Grace, Grig offers him the possibility of human company, care and protection. As in all of his work, Bond is not arguing that beneath the surface veneer of human civilisation lies a primitive, savage human nature. The play is not paradigmatic of Golding's *Lord of the Flies*. Rather, *The Crime of the Twenty-First Century* advocates once again the rational imperative for justice directly associated by Bond with his concept of radical innocence. The play shows that, without the sanity of art and imagination to inform the struggle for justice, only the 'rationale' of the insane atrocities of Auschwitz and in the former Yugoslavia will continue to prevail. The crime of the twenty-first century is the formal, systematic denial – enforced by the use and threatened use of nuclear weapons – of the possibility or need for human society.

Innocence (written 2008, published 2011)

Innocence has not (at the time of writing) been performed. It is set in the later decades of the twenty-first century and in that sense is futuristic. It is dystopian and relates to some extent to Bond's previously discussed *The Crime of the Twenty-First Century*. It explores a remnant of humanity rediscovering and rebuilding itself in the wake of a cataclysmic event. One also feels the reverberations of an even earlier play, *Red Black and Ignorant* (1984), from *The War Plays* trilogy.

However, the significant development and evolution in Bond's dramatic style and form from 1984 is that *Innocence* radically deconstructs and interrogates the ontological phenomena of humanity. *Red Black and Ignorant* represented possibly the last of Bond's mid-career 'solution' plays in its use of an episodic, parabolic form. The differences between the two plays and the almost 25-year journey that paradoxically separates yet connects them are philosophical, ideological and aesthetic.

The characters in *Innocence* range from WAPO deserters (a neo-fascist paramilitary group) through to a small number of civilian survivors of whatever apocalyptic event has devastated human society. The play is structured in two parts. The first four scenes are located in the fens – desolate, flat wetland marshes in the east of England. Given that Bond's parents and forbears came from the Cambridgeshire fens, there is a sense in which the setting might be interpreted as akin to a psycho-political, 'geologically' stratified site of the psychodynamic and the political. The historical 'DNA' of the past intrudes and interacts traumatically with an imagined future redolent of Goya. Scenes 5 to 11, which constitute Part Two, take place almost entirely at a house occupied by the character Son and his partner Grace. Their attempts to rebuild, materially and meta-phorically, a sense of home are disrupted through the arrival of Treg and his travelling partner, Woman. Treg, a former WAPO deserter himself, has escaped from the fens. With a deep if amorally prag-matic instinct for survival and self-preservation, Treg sees all people and places as potential providers for his own needs. Bond's use of archetypal character names such as Son and Woman signals once more a kind of meta-location in the 'later plays' such as *Innocence*, in that they are enacted on a site of radicalised imagination and psychic conflict, which are both material and metaphorical. As is so often the case in the 'later plays' but may also be glimpsed in *The Pope's Wedding* almost 50 years previously, Bond equates the 'dra-matic site' of the human imagination as a layered phenomenology. It soon transpires from the first intrusion of Treg's darkly egocen-tric *modus operandi* that the Woman is the Son's mother. Equally, the significance of Grace's name is revealed as she demonstrates a capacity for selfless empathy in dialectical opposition to Treg's rapacity. It is as if some of the central conflicts and themes of the play are themselves embodiments of neo-Freudian, Oedipal forces. Even as the material reality of the world has been traumatised, so the principal characters are reminiscent of Strindberg's descrip-tions of his own characters as 'scraps and fragments of humanity'. Whereas Scopey in *The Pope's Wedding* had sought to existentially 'put on' the identity of the murdered Alen through the shamanistic wearing of his victim's coat, the Son in *Innocence* seeks his lost self in 'putting on' his Jungian shadow self. His impulse is not only filial but as desperate for both his own sanity and the sanity of human communion:

> SON I'm afraid t'be sick in the 'ead. I want t' be a 'uman being. Just that. In all this shit 'n rubble. (*I*, p. 76)

When his mother and Grace plead with him not to go on a futile search for his brother, the Son replies with a powerful rhetoric of a need born of profound existential despair:

> I'd 'ave t' go even if I didn't want to. Yesterday I didn't know 'e existed. Now I don't want t'live without 'im. 'E's whass bin missin all me life. When I find 'im things'll change. It'll solve everythin. 'E's me only chance. 'E'll tell me why my life's bin wasted. How I should live [...] 'E's like a ghost 'ere. I'll bring 'im back t'live. (*I*, p. 74)

The iconic image of the broken, divided, 'Wounded Man' hovers above and within much of Bond's entire output. The Son's profound sense of alienation, fracture and loss echoes Joe's (in *The Children*) similar existential and moral predicament in his relationship with his mother. In that play this angst is transferred and projected onto Joe's inanimate dummy. Interestingly in both *The Children* and *Innocence* this is a world in which fathers in the socially conventional sense are absent. In these plays, and of course across much of Bond's output, masculinity is frequently delineated in terms of violence and acute emotional and psychological disconnectedness. To the extent that Treg might be interpreted as a meta-father figure, he encapsulates the familiar Bond territory of a premeditated, psychotic self-interest, enforced and realised through the amorality of violence. Treg cannot accommodate or permit the Son to have an autonomous identity and existence independent of him. The Man in *The Children* is driven not only to avenge the death of his son by Joe. In a profound, psychotic double take, in seeking to kill Joe, the Man potentially seeks to murder his own neo-filial son and thus ensure his own psychic integrity and material existence.

In terms of the even more complex semiotics of the character of the Silhouette Soldier and his relationship to the dead baby (and by implication the Son), Bond enters a truly radicalised dramaturgy of a new poetics of political drama.

The Silhouette Soldier experiences an inverse, mirrored version of the Son's alienation and loss. He walks the earth with a baby that he has bayoneted to death. This haunting, harrowing image evokes the myth of Cain, co-first born of 'the first born' in that ancient Judaic ontological narrative. Cain is destined to walk the earth bearing the irremovable, moral stigmata of his killing of his brother Abel. He is 'marked out' for all eternity with a scar that is both material and metaphorical. The Silhouette Soldier searches for a kind of redemption although it's not clear from what he seeks release and liberation. Like the Son, his proto-brother, he mourns and yearns for his lost, fractured other-self:

> Where's me brother? I bin through the village! All the 'ouses! Me feet wore the streets bare! All the locks! Turn the keys! The locks bled [...] Where's me brother? (*I*, p. 82)

The Silhouette Soldier is destined to eternally and repeatedly murder the dead baby in a nightmarish, performative vignette evocative of Auschwitz or My Lai. It is in a dark, deep symbolic sense *both* his brother *and* himself. As the Son is forced to witness the carnal brutality of his divided self, he seeks cathartic release from the Silhouette Soldier in equal measure to his original desire for union. The Son pleads with him to terminate this horror show of twenty-first-century inhumanity against a backdrop of a terrifying evensong of the dead, innocent victims of humanity's history:

> SON Don't want 'im! Don't want me brother!
> SILHOUETTE SOLDIER (*jerks baby on string*) Stab! Stab! Stab! Stab!
> WAPOS (*off*) Mob! Mob! Mob! Mob! Mob!
> SON (*to* WAPO 3) Make 'im stop! Tell 'im! Ain want me brother!
> SILHOUETTE SOLDIER (*looks round. Holds the hanged baby on the string*) Don't want – ? 'Oo said don't want? Don't matter?
> SON Don't 'ang the baby!
> SILHOUETTE SOLDIER 'E must want 'is brother. 'E drag it out a'me – the effort t'get 'is brother – drag half me body out a' me! – now 'e don't want 'im! Hhhuh! (*Falls down*)

DEAD (*crying from the ground*) The baby's dead. The dead weep for their own.

[...]

He stands up with the baby. It is completely black and closer to the human shape – the ball of the head, the stumps of the arms. The longer stumps of the legs burnt together. A charred child from Hiroshima. (*I*, p. 83)

Bond creates simultaneously in the Silhouette Soldier a character that is a profound dialectics of materiality, memory, loss and history. In his final, farewell speech to the Son, the Silhouette Soldier is used by Bond in two respects. The first is to weave a tragic tapestry of the human capacity for violence. The second is history's ideological authorising and legitimising of it for power and exploitation. The Silhouette Soldier embodies the soldiers from the Nazi execution squad in *Coffee*, the young men in scene 6 of *Saved*, and the anonymous men engaged in the 'ethnic cleansing' of 800 Muslim men, women, children and babies killed in one day in the Bosnian War. His and their humanity is our own. Shared. The Son has gone to search for human contact. He has sought a comradeship and communion that might bridge the chasm at the core of his alienated identity. He encounters that fractured other self, not as a brother in arms, but as an embodiment of his own potentiality to kill and maim. In a savage logic born of Hades and Belsen, he is the one authorised to kill the 'other', the outsider, alien and refugee. Instilled and authorised by ideological imperative, the Silhouette Soldier kills those who, ideological propaganda informs him, would kill him and his 'brother':

SILHOUETTE SOLDIER Yer want the truth? This thing on the string'd grow up t'kill yer brother! 'Oo stops it? I stop it so yer can tell me not t'stop it! I'll tell yer the truth! (*Points to the mass grave*) All them I kill – all the layers – in all the wars – the big ones – the dirty little scraps – since they learn the art a' throwin stones at each other's 'eads – me breath accuses me a' murder each time it comes out me mouth! – I'm the purpose of the world! –'n it aint enough! I ain kill enough! Never enough! (*I*, p. 84)

As is often the case in Bond's writing, the fracture and alienation within individual characters and indeed communities are not solely individual/personal nor collective/social. Neither are they simplistically or intrinsically psychological as opposed to sociological. The Silhouette Soldier is a uniquely powerful fusion of dark and seemingly contradictory forces and facets of human identity, society, politics and culture. He is a complex, layered, dialectical dramatic entity. The subjective-psychic imperative struggles in paradoxical collusion-opposition to the external-ideological forces. Out of this dialectic, a character is created who embodies history's human tragedies: its pogroms, crusades and jihads. These tragedies are not the inevitable working-out of an 'intrinsic' human need for violence. They are neither the fatalistic intrusion of Sophocles' gods-as-puppet masters. The competing, destructive dialectics that constitute the Silhouette Soldier are the dynamics of a humanness which is not fixed in some dark, Social Darwinist sense. Bound in a mucous mesh of the dilemmas and imperatives of human identity and morality, 'innocence' can only ever be the 'other side' of the underneath of the human struggle for justice.

Have I None (2000)

Have I None is the third play written in what Bond referred to originally as the 'Big Brum' trilogy. The other two plays are *At the Inland Sea* (1995) and *Eleven Vests* (1997).

In the two earlier plays Bond explores what were to re-emerge as recurring themes in his work from the mid 1990s onwards. They had their origins in earlier work, however. One of these themes is the mother–son relationship. This is not to presuppose or impose a simplistic neo-Freudian reading of those relationships and the plays in which they occur. Rather it is to acknowledge and explore the importance of the complex need for care and nurturing in the emergence of the 'human'.

For example, in *At the Inland Sea*, the play's dynamics centre upon two relationships. They are both between an adolescent boy and an older woman. One is a mother–son relationship and the other is a relationship between the boy and a woman and her baby from Auschwitz who are about to perish in the gas chambers (Figure 1). Bond creates and explores parallels between the moral imperative that the 'historical' Woman places upon the boy, with the confused and conflicting emotional expectations between the boy and his own mother. The Woman tells the boy that if he tells a story to her

Figure 1   Mandy Finney in the role of Woman in *At the Inland Sea*, which was the first commissioned play from Bond by Big Brum in 1995, directed by Geoff Gillham. The photograph powerfully conveys the tragic vulnerability embodied by this character, who with her baby is an internee of a Nazi concentration camp. Like Joe in *The Children*, a character known only as Boy is experiencing conflict at home with his mother and anxious about his imminent school examinations. It is out of these tensions that the Woman appears in the Boy's bedroom with her baby, distraught and frightened but determined to survive. Her life-and-death command to the Boy is a challenging moral imperative: 'Tell me a story. Then my baby will live' (*AIS*, p. 11)

and her dying baby that they will survive. He therefore becomes in a mysterious way the origin and redemptive means of their actual and continuing existence. The boy embarks upon a harrowing journey of not only self-discovery but also, crucially, a discovery of the world.

Even as this life-changing journey leads into the possibility of a more mature co-equal relationship with his mother and the possibility of rapprochement, the moral and existential dilemmas which he has faced echo Joe's anguished question to the puppet in scene 1 of *The Children*, 'Am I supposed to change the world?'

Perhaps the crucial difference between *At the Inland Sea* and *Eleven Vests* and *Have I None* is the context in which setting, characterisation and narrative are delineated and explored. In *Eleven Vests*, Bond revisits familiar thematic territory in interrogating with its attendant criminality contrasts with the ideologically legitimised violence of soldiers murdering enemy hostages.

Whilst those two earlier plays in the trilogy are characterised by recognisable settings and characters (albeit in *At the Inland Sea* the present being invaded by the past), *Have I None* creates a world in which the past has been abolished by an unnamed but authoritarian regime. As Jams, a member of a state-authorised, uniformed paramilitary group, observes to his wife and a stranger, Grit, who has arrived at their home claiming to be Sara's long-lost brother:

> JAMS Authority was right to abolish the past. Get shot of it. Videos-tapes-discos-dressing up-raves-dot com dot-junk. People were sick with it. It was a hobby to buy a new car, drive away from the sales-room and crash it into a wall. What do people do when they've got everything? One day they beg you to take it away. They want peace instead. That's why they grab at resettlement – why it's easy to forget. (*HIN*, p. 79)

On one level the play is a strange, intriguingly provocative evocation of iconic objects from Bond's work. A chair assumes a meta-theatricality and iconic significance in this play where the material world has been stripped not only of its past but also of any substantial present. Len's chair, which embodied a provisional optimism, has now taken on a fetishised commoditisation, with Jams and his wife fighting and arguing over the identity and ownership of the two chairs in their otherwise barren home. The chairs are themselves tangible, material indicators and symptoms of a world in which, robbed of their past and the relative coherence that provided for their identities and lives, spontaneous mass suicides are happening in the world outside. Grit explains to Jams after he arrives that 'the other end of the country', his former home, is a form of hell above the earth:

> GRIT Nothing worked. No jobs. No electricity [...] On the way to work I had to cross a bridge. Crowd on it. Sitting and standing both sides on the parapets. Done up in overcoats. Looked like rows of pigeons – roosting or walking up and down looking for a place. Then one of them'd throw theirself in the river. That started it. Splash-splash-splash. Five or six throw themselves in. Others climb up to fill the gaps they left. The ones in the river float off. (*HIN*, p. 62)

There are further haunting images of human beings so traumatised and alienated that they spontaneously embark upon a frenzy of self-harm and violent suicide. Placing these incidents in the geographical location of a real urban location of Reading only amplifies their nightmarish meta-reality:

> JAMS Know Reading?
> GRIT No.
> JAMS Place down this end. Suburb before it was resettled. They had an outbreak [...] They walked down the streets carrying a knife in front of them – like this. (*He holds his fork at arm's length*) Point up. Hundreds of 'em. Streets were chocker. Going up and down. Like sleepwalkers holding a candle out. Dead quiet. No one spoke [...] All of a sudden one of 'em'd stab theirself. Stab stab stab [...] As if they wanted to stab themselves as many times as they could before the knife fell out of their hand. Never stabbed anyone else. (*HIN*, p. 63)

In a world where the past has been abolished, there can be no present, or at least its validity and meaning are traumatically compromised. Thus when Sara arrives home to find Grit present – a man who claims to be her brother and carries with him a photograph of themselves as children – it's as if the past erupts like an ontological and psycho-emotional earthquake.

The three characters descend into a dark, dangerous game of accusation, recrimination and denial. It is a world punctuated by knocks on the door of the house and yet no person or persons ever being visible when the door is answered. The past knocks and yet, whilst heard – a distant, nostalgic, troubling echo – cannot be seen. When it can, through some seismic faultline of time and memory, then it must be denied and, ultimately, destroyed. In destroying the past, the present simultaneously writes its own suicide note.

Scene 3 of the play centres upon an encounter exploring the relationship between Grit and Sara. It is characterised by both the complex visual semiotic signs employed by Bond in terms of Sara's costume and the equally complex layering of past and present, memory and truth. As with many of the scenes in this play, scene 3 begins with a knock on the door which, on being answered by Grit, reveals no one there. When the door opens immediately after, it is Sara who enters. Her costume and appearance are described thus:

> She wears a ground-length loose coat of stiff sky-blue silk. It is cov-
> ered with metal spoons. They are stitched to the silk so they cannot
> swing loosely but can knock against each other when the coat moves.
> (*HIN*, p. 23)

This costume can be interpreted as evoking the blue of the sky or sea – vast natural expansive locations – in tension with the problematised proximity of the oppressive domestic site which Sara inhabits. In terms of visual dialectics the costume evokes therefore a material aesthetic which transcends and yet is simultaneously trapped by the angry 'shout' of Sara's 'present' with the more elusive 'call' of her 'past'.

Having previously denied any prior knowledge or recollection of Grit when he claims to be her brother, Sara now embarks upon a ritual litany of memory couched amongst some of Bond's most beautiful, muscular poetics:

> SARA In the night I came to the room where they put you. You
> were in a coma. I held my hand over your head [...] There were
> drops all over your face. I thought that was fever: your skin
> cried [...] So I pulled back the blanket – you smelt like a stable
> on a frosty night – and dragged you to the window so that you
> could see. It was dark. The glass was black. I saw your face in
> it. It was white. Your face was talking to you. I couldn't hear it.
> (*HIN*, p. 77)

The interplay of the bleak materiality of disease and mortality inter-woven with the evocation of that materiality embodying its own self-reflexive, poetic transcendence – 'skin cried', 'a stable on a frosty night', 'Your face was talking to you' – is powerful and potent. There is a carefully constructed, creative collision in this iconic dramatic memory of a face that 'talks' to its owner through its meta-reflection. It evokes the relationship of the puppet to Joe in *The Children*. The signified 'inanimate' and 'materialist' entity is invested with life, identity and volition by the alienated, divided self who seeks an integrated coherence through the externalised Other.

Fleetingly Sara and Grit are able to experience a moment of a shared past and a shared present of rest and peace: 'You are my sister. I remember my face in the window.' This remembered filial, fragile Eden is shattered by the violent intrusion of Jams, which is powerfully, visually pre-signed by Sara taking off her coat and put-ting it back on again. 'The inside is black and covered with bones.' The costume embodies its own destructive dialectic and conflict. Simultaneously, shaman-like, it turns in upon itself to pre-empt Jam's entry characterised by his paranoiac survival instinct:

> JAMS Chriss – another burden [...] If her body had turned up and hadn't been reported absent – I'd be censured. If I can't find her or tell her a good story: chop. (*HIN*, p. 25)

Sara leaves as Jams ties Grit to a chair. In his subsequent speech Jams reveals the existential insecurity underpinning his desperate anxiety to affirm the power, policies and ideology of the authoritarian regime named only as 'the service':

> The suffering will end. There's still the odd lunatic. The old women with pictures in their heads. The stray kids. *I'm* not immune to it – some days I feel like the footprint in the land where no man has trod. But still it gets less. The suffering goes. (*HIN*, p. 79)

In a society where the past has been abolished, the present must be controlled into some semblance of purpose and coherence through violence, fear and intimidation. This drives Jams, and seemingly Sara too, to conspire to poison Grit with the portion of soup she has made for him. If Grit, the intruder from and as the past, can be destroyed, then the nightmarish version of a present reality can surely be resurrected and sustained by the dysfunctional couple. In a final sequence that is characterised by a darkly savage, almost farcical humour of ruse, subterfuge, counter-subterfuge and bowls of soup suffering an identity crisis, Jams is left alone, finally and utterly disempowered of his last remnant of a hope that was as poisonous and deadly as the soup intended for Grit. Howling and distraught, and with no ethical or existential compass to steer the chaotic present collapsing around him, he attempts to leave only to return with a dystopian utterance worthy of Macbeth's vision of the ghost of Banquo: 'Oh God it's worse than Reading.' In terms of the multi-textured complexities as a dystopian political allegory and the finely crafted interfacing of the alienated yet symbiotic inner-personal and outer-public identities, *Have I None* represents an important way-mark in the evolution of the 'later plays'.

'The Birmingham Plays'

The Children (2000)

What is remarkable about this play in terms of its creative inception is the defining meta-presence of *Medea* by Euripides. With its central preoccupation of the complex relationship between a mother and her children, it is also the inspiration for Bond's most recent work at the time of writing (March 2012) – *Dea*. Bond intended that *There Will Be More*, commissioned for the season of six plays at the Cock Tavern Theatre (Kilburn, London) in 2010, would represent the first in what would evolve eventually as a trilogy of plays under the one title. In the epigraph of the published edition of *The Children*, in conjunction with *Have I None*, Bond quotes as follows from *Medea*:

> CHILD O help, help!
>   Where can I go to escape? (Bond, 2000a)

These words and sentiments evoke the existential and ethical dilemma facing the central character of Joe, a teenage boy, in the play. By implication it also haunts the other children of the play's title. They are Joe's friends and share the same bleak material and emotional environment of Joe and his mother. There is also a powerful sense in which the themes of psychological distress and physical danger summon up the suffering of all children throughout history exposed to exploitation and degradation.

In the alienation and despair of Joe's relationship with the puppet and his mother, we are perhaps reminded of the young men in *Saved* who, in killing the baby, are, at an ontological level, also killing themselves. The violence of the world, it might be argued, transmutes its causes of social and political inequality and injustice. Like a deadly virus, perhaps, it infects and destroys the young men in the park and Joe.

In addition to the summer riots of 2011, the abduction and murder of the two-year-old James Bulger in February 1993 by two schoolboys, Robert Thompson and Jon Venables, hovered over this author's production of *The Children* in 2012. The reporting of this case in the reactionary right-wing media took on a grotesque and voyeuristic ugliness of its own. The dreadful tragedy of an infant victim taken from a crowded shopping mall, the New Strand Shopping Centre in Bootle near Liverpool, to a deserted railway track and subjected to the most appalling torture and killing by Thompson and Venables fuelled an explosion of Neolithic tabloid rage. In a programme note that Bond wrote specially for my own 2012 production of *The Children* with an undergraduate cast from the University of Winchester, performed at the Winchester Theatre Royal, the dramatist observed:

The opening of *The Children* relates to the murder of a toddler, James Bulger, by two young children. The murder caused a flare-up of plague symptoms in the press and the police – two institutions that, it seems, share an illegal cash symbiosis. There was talk of evil and internment for life. When I wrote the play I remember what happened when the two children were driven from court. Lines of police held back a screaming kicking fist-waving mob. A man broke through and hammered at the side of the police van. He screamed in the most violent language that the two children should be hanged. Government ministers use different phrases but with the same purport – a diagnostic symptom of this plague is the corruption of public discourse. Children are probably the one group in our society who are not carriers of the parasite bacillus. They are its victims. A society gets the children it creates.

There is a disturbing anonymity in the naming of the boy who is killed by Joe when he sets fire to the house as the Stranger, which is also reflected in the namelessness of Joe's puppet. Killer and the killed, the animate and the inanimate, are intertwined in a tragic, triangular violence born of incubated alienation in the mute figure of the puppet belonging to Joe in *The Children* (Figure 2). This puppet has no strings in any literal sense. As an inanimate, iconic model of commodified value and control, its strings might be defined as the workings of mass-mediated consumer capitalism. In terms of the stage drama it relies for its existence upon Joe's imagination and

Figure 2 Josh Moody playing the central role of Joe in the University of Winchester production at the Theatre Royal Winchester 2012 of *The Children*, directed by Peter Billingham. Joe is seen pensively holding the puppet which is dressed in clothes that suggest a school uniform. Its size is about half that of the actor. Joe talks to the puppet as if it were real and shortly after this moment in the play his complex feelings towards it explode when he batters it to a symbolic death with a brick. There are disturbing connotations in this action reminiscent of the murder of James Bulger, aged two, by two older boys in 1993. Joe's traumatic feelings and actions mirror his inner conflict and also his relationship with his mother. Joe says to the puppet just before he attacks it: 'Anything goes wrong in our house Mum hits me. Don't know why. Am I supposed to change the world?' (*TC*, p. 6)

actions. In this respect the etymological origin of the word 'inspire' is to 'breathe in' or, more actively, 'breathe life'. In this significant sense the puppet is 'inspired' into 'life' through the troubled waters of Joe's imagination. From Bond's perspective, this 'imagination' is not of the post-Romantic autonomous and ethereal variety. Rather Joe's imagination has its existence and context within the socio-cultural and psychological nexus of his relationship with his mother. In its sombre muteness the puppet is as vulnerable to and dependent upon the manipulation of other, external human agency as is the baby in its pram in *Saved*. Equally Joe is subject to the complex strategies of emotional blackmail and psychological manipulation from his dysfunctional mother. With dark resonance of the James Bulger case, the puppet is also subjected by Joe and the other children to a tortured stoning with bricks. It is as if Jung's 'Shadow Self' in fusion with Marx's concept of the fetishised and commodified human being are woven into one disturbing, iconic image of alienation and violence.

In the opening scene of the play Joe enters alone save for the puppet, which is dressed in a costume that suggests a school uniform. Significantly the setting is an abandoned lot by a railway line. This setting, in a desolate urban location, evokes those tragic train journeys in which the Jews were transported to their mass deaths in the Nazi concentration camps. The troubled existence invested in the puppet by Joe is a dark metaphor of Joe's own profound sense of his fractured identity. The aura of alienation informs Joe's conversation with the puppet, which is an ontological discourse with his Jungian shadow self:

> JOE Why do I drag you around? You get me into trouble. Didn't go to school today because of you. Mum won't have you in the house anymore [...] Sometimes I hear myself talk and think it's you. Anyone listening now would think I'm mad [...] It's not my fault you're not real [...] I told you everything I didn't tell anyone else [...] I'll have to kill you. (*TC*, pp. 5–6)

Joe proceeds to attack the puppet with bricks from the derelict site even as the stage directions indicate that he 'Half-hugs and play-fully half-swings it from side to side'. Joe's anguished recognition of his psychic confusion in relation to his puppet and his power over it – to destroy or save – is potent. It is further explored in the disturbing mirrored proximity of his relationship with his mother. Like so many of Bond's working-class female characters, stretching back to Mary and Pam in *Saved*, Joe's mother is torn between the crushing disappointments of daily life and a desire to exercise some form of desperate self-empowerment. Her endemic sense of life's emotional impotency and material deprivation is conveyed within moments of Joe returning home in scene 2. There is a perverse game playing in her displacement and denial of pleasure through cigarettes and an aborted night out with a boyfriend:

> MOTHER [...] I expect you've been with your mates. Nice time?
> JOE (*confused*) Well.
> MOTHER Enjoy yourself your age. There isn't much enjoyment later.
> JOE (*misunderstanding*) I stopped you going out.
> MOTHER Didn't really want to. Didn't have the energy to dress up. Hard day at work. You gave me an excuse to stay in. Your tea's in the micro. Just needs switching on. (*TC*, p. 7)

When Joe subsequently confesses that he has 'lost' the money that his mother had given him to buy cigarettes ('fags') for her, the strained civility of her initial response catapults into open, bitter recrimination:

> JOE I lost your fag money.
> MOTHER O? How?
> JOE Lost it.
> MOTHER (*irritated*) You can't have 'lost it'! Look in your pockets.
> JOE Have.
> MOTHER Look again. People don't just lose things. I had to work for that. I don't sit in a chair all day or make myself a nuisance hanging round bus shelters. (*TC*, p. 8)

Joe's guilt is entrenched in his secret shame that he has used her money to buy sweets for the puppet. This connotation of oral pleasure as gratification between his mother's need for cigarettes and Joe's need for sweets is displaced through the puppet as inanimate desire swirls with other complex feelings.

Like some problematic modern-day Medea, the mother proceeds in this same scene to tell Joe that she has a special favour and task to ask of him. In Euripides' *Medea*, first performed in 431 BC and which won third prize at the City Dionysia, the play's narrative centres on the ultimate revenge of a wronged woman on her treacherous lover, Jason. Medea's vendetta culminates in her killing of their children in order to cause him irreparable suffering. In *The Children*, the play's title clearly and pointedly removes the dramatic and ethical focus of attention away from the wronged woman and mother to the children. Crucially it is Joe who is commanded by his mother – as evidence of his love and loyalty to her – to burn down a house recently built on a nearby new estate. Joe is as distraught and split by his mother's demands as the puppet has been by the traumatic, paradoxical counterclaims of affection and hatred metered out upon it by Joe. When Joe asks 'Why? Who lives there? I won't ask anything else', his mother responds with a nightmarish logic. She asserts that although it's not wrong 'it's against the law'. She then exerts a perverse moral authority to the proposed act by asserting: 'If you knew the circumstances I'm shielding you from – you'd say burning wasn't drastic enough!' Through a psychologically complex, manipulative emotional dynamics she affirms a subsidiary moral value of the act as 'This will keep us together. Bring us closer.' When Joe subsequently consummates these conflicting filial demands through setting fire to the house, identifiable only by its mauve door, his mother responds with anger and disbelief:

> JOE Mum you told me to do – !
> MOTHER Stop it! Stop it! [...] Told you to burn a house? What mother would tell her child to do that? She'd be a monster!
> (*TC*, p. 22)

Bond's construction of the character of Joe's mother locates her simultaneously as oppressed both in her internalised psycho-emotional realm and under the social and economic pressures of being a poor, white, working-class woman. Furthermore, in the penultimate scene of the play – as identified later in this discussion of *The Children* – we discover that she has been dehumanised and commodified in her working role as a prostitute earlier in her life. Crucially, that experience seems to precede Joe's birth. The dual impact of her primary cash-value as a prostitute resonates in her anger and guilt towards Joe: 'If I'd thought like you, you'd have ended up in the pedal bin of an abortion clinic.' Her acutely diminished and destructive self-esteem descends into a paralysing self-hatred. This is presented by Bond as central to the violence of the narrative arc of her vengeance against her former pimp, the Man, through the agency of her son. Her self-hatred defines her dysfunctional relationship with her son in a powerful way whilst also revealing a perverse logic and rationale to her actions and relationship with her son. In a letter to Rosa López de D'Amico, dated 20 March 1993, Bond wrote:

> Why so many of my women characters are more politically active and aware than many of my men characters is not because I wish specifically to deal with feminist questions. I find that to consider almost any contemporary political problem from a woman's point of view throws more light on it. Radicalises the problem. (Bond, 1994–2000, vol. 2, p. 196)

Whilst Joe's mother is not of course an active agent of radicalised political change, she may nevertheless be viewed as potently symptomatic of the wider social, cultural and economic marginalisation of women: especially those of the working class. Bond observes in the same letter:

> I wished to show the cultural and therefore moral destitution of consumer society. In the West – and now in Eastern Europe – left-wing politics have been unable to understand the situation, needs and outlooks of ordinary people who live in an affluent society [...] for them affluence creates a very paradoxical state of affairs. (p. 195)

In order to fully understand the complex character and dramatic function of Joe's mother in *The Children*, Bond understands that she needs to be viewed within a corrosive dialectic of her psychological trauma as a woman in a contested site with her class status as an oppressed working-class woman. This 'visibility' of her alienated and self-destructive 'need' can only be more completely understood against the 'invisibility' of late consumer capitalism's strategies of power and subordination.

Having engaged in a collective bonding ritual of the stoning of the puppet prior to this scene, Joe and the other children realise that they have to escape from the consequences of the arson attack. This requires that they embark on a journey away from the known and into an increasingly decaying, traumatised unknown world beyond their homes. These homes themselves are characterised by their own localised suffering: 'My mum can't cope in her wheelchair [...] My old man drinks' (*TC*, p. 29).

Images of some wider, even global catastrophe begin to quietly saturate their awareness of the world and each other as they journey through a landscape of apocalyptic devastation. This sense of isolation and vulnerability is movingly conveyed in the following dialogue from scene 7:

> FRIENDS We're lost. Like being shipwrecked in the empty fields. Why've they knocked the houses down? We don't know where we are. We don't know where we're going. What we're doing. What'll become of us? (*TC*, p. 35)

Catechised into a maturity beyond his years by his tragically misplaced expression of loyalty and love for his mother, it is Joe who articulates the moral imperative of caring for the seemingly vulnerable and displaced Man (Figure 3):

> JOE It's like walking off and leaving us at our own funeral [...] When he can walk he can choose what he does. I think he's the only thing keeping us together. After all this, if we could walk off and leave someone to starve to death – what's the point of anything? If there was only *me* left – I still wouldn't leave him. (*TC*, pp. 39–40)

Their harrowing journey, with its implicit cycle of death and violent revenge, is ultimately punctuated by two crucial and significant moments. The first refers to the Stranger extending forgiveness to Joe, his unwitting murderer. The audience has previously seen the Stranger in scene 3 of the play when he comes accidentally upon Joe and the gang, with a fight ensuing. When the Stranger appears in scene 11, he is dressed in exactly the same costume as the puppet who has been collectively and ritually stoned to 'death' by Joe and his friends. This blurring of the identities of the puppet and

Figure 3   Josh Moody and Emily Maloney as Joe and his friend Jill in the University of Winchester production of *The Children* directed by Peter Billingham (2012). Joe, Jill and some of their other friends have fled from their home after Joe tells them that he has set fire to a house on order from his mother in which a boy has burnt to death. They are travelling through a desolate post-apocalyptic landscape and on the way take pity on a Man who seems to be destitute and in need of care. When the others want to leave the Man behind, Joe says to Jill: 'After all this, if we could walk off and leave someone to starve to death – what's the point of anything?' (*TC*, p. 40)

the Stranger simultaneously reflects Joe's troubled relationship to both. There is a haunting reverberation in the reappearance of the Stranger, who was killed through Joe's act of fractured, Oedipally displaced arson, and the visual identity of the puppet. After reliving and describing to Joe his immolation in the burning house, the Stranger confronts Joe's guilt in a profoundly unexpected and moving way:

JOE I could have called the fireman sooner.
STRANGER I know.
JOE I ran along the ditch. Tripped over the rat.
STRANGER I came to forgive you.
JOE Forgive me?
STRANGER Yes you didn't mean to kill me (*TC*, p. 51)

This iconic encounter embodies a critical marker in Joe's geo-existential journey. His new-found capacity for self-forgiveness and acceptance is predicated on his loyalty and care for the Man. That the Man is in fact Joe's Oedipal nemesis only deepens the dramatic power of the subsequent and penultimate scene of the play.

The Man, on whom the children have taken initially begrudging pity, is revealed by Bond with a terrifying, tragic denouement to be the avenging, murderous judgement of a marginalised, contemporary 'Jason'. It transpires that the dead boy, the Stranger, was in fact the Man's son. Furthermore, in his final anguished speech, the Man makes a climactic revelation:

> MAN My son's dead! Your mother was a whore. She worked for me. I kept the money. Bought the house. She wanted to move in with me. No! I moved in with my wife! Your mother wanted revenge! She burnt the house! (*Gestures*) They only *knew* – the ones I killed! You *did* it! You killed my son! (*TC*, p. 51)

This constitutes the second critical moment in the play's climax and denouement. In a drama borne out of classically tragic proportions, Joe is seen as much at the mercy of a pre-existing Fate and others' contested desires, jealousies and rage as the puppet is of his own conflicted feelings. In that powerful sense Joe and indeed the Stranger may be seen as thematic equivalents to the puppet. The dramatic territory of the play assumes a psychic dimension and this is a deep and enduring characteristic of many of the 'later plays'. It is not of course that the social, economic and political context of the play is secondary or redundant. Rather it is in the fusion of the external with the internal elements of the play that Bond's dramatic vision enters a distinctive, defining phase. It would be misleadingly simplistic to assert that there is an irretrievable osmosis between the psychology and the sociology of the characters in *The Children*. What Bond achieves is a much more significant and complex synthesis of the imagination-as-dramatic-site with a materiality of human history that is self-reflexive. There is a co-existent totality of meaning between a dialectical vision of history and a Marxist perspective with a metaphor of reflexive transcendence located in Kant's concept of that which can only be known through the noumenal in tension with the moral imperative. The materiality of the puppet is therefore

not defined solely by its constituent elements but embodies a profound poetics of being and knowing empowered and animated by
the psycho-imaginative impulse of drama itself.

In the play's final scene Joe is left alone at the end of his, and the
play's, journey. He has nothing in terms of the festishised 'ownership'
of capitalism, having relinquished the temptation of unlimited consumer goods brought about by the devastation and looting that has
fallen upon the world. His painful but redemptive and transformative
journey has brought him a precious and priceless wisdom and insight:
the enduring human need for contact and communion – 'I've got
everything. I'm the last person in the world. I must find someone.
(*Goes*)' (*TC*, p. 52).

In this moving, complex poetic parable from the first century of
the new millennium, and almost 40 years on from *Saved*, it's as if Len
who struggled to repair the chair as an expression of the 'optimism
for optimism' has a progeny in Joe. Whilst the social, political and
economic world of Len's inception might be beyond repair, Joe and
the radical imagination that authorised his creation nevertheless see
the making of our progressive and revolutionary humanness as the
only path forward. The moral imperative of this can only be realised
in the competing and destructive politics of inequality and exploitation in the early twenty-first century. Bond stated in the Introduction
to the *Chair Plays*:

> Does 'man' survive? Prometheus turned into Epimetheus, the
> man who unknowingly brought destruction and chaos into the
> world. He is the satanic demiurge of the capitalism that does
> not know itself and that creates ecological catastrophe. Men and
> women have their humanness in common but perhaps in the
> new drama the immanent transcendent must be created first by
> women. Transcendence is the story of radical innocence and it has
> no end. (2012a, p. xiii)

Tune (2007)

Commissioned and first staged by Big Brum on 22 February 2007,
Tune was directed by Chris Cooper. I was able to see a performance of
the play as part of the At the Sharp End symposium on contemporary
British theatre and playwriting organised at the University of Portsmouth in September 2008.

Bond's note for the setting reveals once more his ongoing and increasing exploration of the materiality of set and location as embodying and expressing a meta-poetic materiality:

> *A room. The back wall appears to be solid but is made of malleable material such as cloth. Behind it is another wall which exactly resembles the first wall but is solid. A kitchen table and chair, both wood. (T, p. 154)*

There is once more a dialectical materiality present and immanent in the wall that is not a wall, which simultaneously interrogates the 'solid' materiality of the further upstage wall. This is not simply a postmodern aesthetic of referenced or multiple materiality but rather a dramatic echoing of the imaginative dimension of the material and the materiality of the imagination. This culminates to deceptively simple but powerful effect in the play as it unfolds within its setting. It is especially the case in terms of the relationship between Robert, a boy, and the Girl, a rough sleeper, whom he befriends. This relationship itself exists in complex emotional and psychological symbiosis with Robert's relationship with Sally, his mother. One of the most telling and intriguing preoccupations of Bond's writing in the 'later plays' is this dynamic between sons and their mothers. It is a rich furrow and Bond returns again and again to excavate its many interrelated strata: emotional, social and political.

Sally is herself torn between the demands of her boyfriend or partner Vernon and her maternal concerns towards her son. It is clear at the start of the play that Robert has withdrawn into a worrying solitude. There is a clear subtext that Robert's silence and withdrawal from the social psychological world of his home are themselves a symptom of his complex emotional anxiety:

> SALLY He won't talk
> VERNON (*starts to go to Robert's room*) I'll have a word with him.
> SALLY No no better not.
> VERNON Kids that age never happy less they're making everyone else miserable. Ignore him. He'll come out when he's hungry.
> SALLY He can be very stubborn.
> VERNON It's me.
> SALLY He hasn't said.

VERNON I thought it was best if we took it slowly. Give him time to get used to seeing me round the house. Hasn't worked. Best I moved in now. He'll have to lump it. (*T*, p. 156)

A series of violent acts of vandalism start to happen which Robert is blamed for. The underlying conflicts of jealousy and rage that might be provoking these acts emanate in an aura of anxiety from Sally:

SALLY You've got a grudge against him. He can't get anything right [...] What am I supposed to believe? Robert I'm asking you to help me. Since your father died I've depended on you for everything. I lived for you till Verny came. That wasn't fair. I put a strain on you. A woman can't depend on a child. It's her job to protect. (*T*, p. 161)

This tangled web of guilt at her subliminally displaced emotional and quasi-sexual dependency is symptomatic of the collapse of the stability of her social and psychological reality. In scene 4, following the smashing up of the conservatory that Vernon has bought for Sally (blamed again upon Robert), the boy metamorphoses into the wall that has separated Vernon from him. At the climactic apex of a litany of mutual recrimination between the quasi-father interloper and Robert, the stage direction says 'The wall collapses into Robert's shape. He comes forward as the wall-figure.'

In this moment of astounding fusion whereby scenic materiality invests the previously unseen Robert with visibility, Robert slowly and inexorably enters a new awareness of himself and his world. The material setting of his existence merges in deep dialectical relationship with an inseparable and mutual ontological reality. In so doing, Bond's concepts of radical innocence and the dramatic site take on a tangible reality. The strata of that transformative site are seen to be not abstract or reductively phenomenological; rather, Robert-Wall and Wall-Robert are viewed as an explosive insight into a revolutionary hybridity of dramatic action with the interrogation of the complex politics of their relationship. In that crucial sense it is a critical dialectical motif of the transformative journey that Bond has taken from the 'aggro-effects' of the earlier plays through to the defining formalism of his concept of the 'theatre event'. Brecht had developed and explored the concept of the 'alienation effect' as a means of disrupting and exposing the false consciousness of socio-cultural and political cohesion of capitalist culture. Bond, through the irrepressible evolution and disciplining of his dramatic vision and craft, has scaled and achieved a new and fundamentally different methodology of politicised performance.

Robert, like Joe in *The Children*, reaps a traumatic reward for his decision to confront the oppressive emotional and psychological regime of adult lives within a neo-nuclear family. The explosive moment of his embryonic ritual passage into the problematic and previously foreign territory of adult life is expressed in his noumenal transformation into and of his psycho-material existence. It is only as Robert emerges out of this rite of passage that he can begin to truly see. This is expressed with powerful dramatic economy in the context of the revelation of Vernon as the *agent provocateur* of the violence that has fallen upon and infected the family and their home:

> *Silence.* VERNON *chews and stares at* ROBERT.
>
> ROBERT (*flat. Realises*) You broke the windscreen.
> VERNON (*nods*) I said sorry car and smashed it with a hammer.
> (*T*, p. 164)

Vernon stabs Robert with a piece of broken glass from the smashed conservatory, a ritual wounding whose echo reverberates like the fork that Vernon has stabbed into the table. The erect, quivering fork, an aggressive psycho-phallic movement, resounds with echoes of Scopey's re-dressing of the murdered Alen, and the exit of the gang from the park after they have killed the baby: their subliminal murmuring borne on the air like the 'buzzing of bees'.

Sally herself remains blinded by denial and tragically compromised by the incessant demands of hardship and desperation. She can only interpret the truth that Robert seeks to share as lies. 'Now you ask me to lie to you. It'd be wrong. Life isn't meant to be easy.' Like Joe's mother in *The Children*, an 'I inherited poverty' adult existence is characterised by remorseless need. Like the hero of an epic, Homeric voyage, Robert sets sail from home, physically and emotionally wounded yet empowered through the ordeal to embark upon his own journey. His travels take him not to the Aegean Sea but the even more troubled waters of living rough on the streets.

In the final scene of play he encounters a girl who tries unsuccessfully to play a musical pipe. Both have run away from traumatic family lives. Robert tells her:

> ROBERT Everything changed. Everything was in my hands. They couldn't hurt me after that. I could have done anything. I *was* the wall. (*T*, p. 173)

As it seems that the girl is going to walk away and leave him, he reiterates, as much for himself as for her, 'It doesn't last – it doesn't have to. I felt it. It happened.'

It is only in his painfully transformed state that Robert can challenge his new friend in an equivalent way to that with which he had tried to open his mother's eyes. The girl has a red blanket which she fantasises burns like a fire to comfort and warm her. Robert's enhanced ontological, existential vision sees and understands the limits of imagined materiality and the profound, radical reimagining of what is real through encounter with the real:

> ROBERT It's a colour ... that's all ... only that. (*Quietly. Desperately*) A colour can't. It doesn't. Can't. Doesn't. It's not like the wall. The wall was *in* me. This is – . A colour doesn't. It can't. (*T*, pp. 175-6)

The play then ends with Robert realising his vision in action by travelling onwards with her to no certain resolution or hope. Robert knows there is no going back for either of them in any sense of the word. His faith is a vulnerable but pragmatic knowledge that their journey must continue and that only they can walk that path: 'We'll find a shelter. Go somewhere [...] Find somewhere' (*T*, p. 176).

The Under Room (2005)

The Under Room is one of three 'later plays' which Bond grouped into a trilogy he called 'The Chair Plays' (with *Chair* and *Have I None*) for the short season of those three works at The Lyric Studio, Hammersmith, London in April/May 2012. The trilogy was divided into a double bill of *Have I None* and *The Under Room*, which opened the season, to be joined by *Chair* in the final part of the run.

The Under Room is set, like its two sister plays, in a foreseeable but futuristic Britain of 2077. The play has the one setting of a basement cellar in a building that contains blocks of flats. The cellar has one flight of steps rising out of it up to an unseen 'over-ground' of a society in a state of cataclysmic unrest and chaos. Crime and civil disorder are rampant, and a repressive government regime employs the army and state terror to try and enforce political and social order (Figure 4).

Into this situation has entered a character called the Dummy Actor who is, as a character, an illegal immigrant on the run from the authorities. It is the unfolding of this character's narrative and back story which acts as the dramaturgical spine of the play. As in other 'later plays' such as *The Children* (previously discussed in this chapter), the play makes use of a dummy as an inanimate prop, described by Bond in the play's stage directions as 'a basic human effigy: trunk, arms, legs, head. It has no other features [...] It is about half the size of The Dummy Actor.' Bond also states in the same stage directions that 'The Dummy Actor speaks the Dummy's words.' This dramatic and staging device is used by Bond in order to explore ideas of alienation and identity and the dialectic between the absence and creation of humanness. Significantly, the other two characters in the play – Joan, who lives in the flat belonging to the cellar, and Jack, who is a figure on the margins of what constitutes law and order and criminality in the world of the play – only ever speak and respond to the Dummy as an inanimate object. They never look at or acknowledge in any sense the Dummy Actor who speaks the Dummy's words.

The Dummy Actor, who says he is a shoplifter, has entered Joan's flat, as he explains to her, to hide from the soldiers who, if they had seen him, would have questioned him and asked to see his official papers which he does not possess. Understandably Joan initially does not believe his story:

> DUMMY If the soldiers stopped me in the streets they would take me away. I have no papers. That is why I broke your window. It was the nearest window. I give you money to buy a new window. You may keep the rest if you wish.
> JOAN Why did you say shoplifting?
> DUMMY It is the truth.
> JOAN It isn't called shoplifting any more. That's what our parents called it. It's shoplooting.
> DUMMY Yes. I know. I forgot. Looting.
> JOAN You were not born here?

Figure 4 Richard Holmes, foreground, as Jack and Adam Bethlenfalvy as Dummy Actor in Big Brum's production of *The Under Room* directed by Chris Cooper. The photograph also shows the Dummy, an inanimate, anonymous figure which is about half the size of the Dummy Actor. In a most interesting and parallel way to the character of Joe and the puppet in *The Children* the Dummy embodies the inner conflicts and emotions of a young illegal economic immigrant who has entered the home of the character Joan for safety. Whilst initially convinced that he has broken into her home as a thief, she slowly believes his tragic story and seeks to help him. This leads to her contacting Jack who, amongst other things, is a courier or trafficker helping people to escape from the ruling military regime – for a price: ''E's incurred obligations. 'E leave 'ere without payin 'e'll 'ave a knife through 'is ribs' (*UR*, p. 185). The Dummy Actor is invisible to Jack and Joan but they respond to his dialogue even as their dramatic focus is upon the Dummy itself. This conveys an enhanced sense of the Dummy's alienated condition both from them and within himself.

> DUMMY When the soldiers took me away they would see me on CCTV from the shops. They would check because I have no papers.
> JOAN You broke into my flat to steal. I came back before you had time.
> DUMMY You do not believe me. If I knew the soldiers had left the street I would have left your house. I meant to pay for the broken window. (*UR*, p. 172)

Joan slowly but surely begins to listen carefully to the intruder and is prepared to accept his account of events. In doing so his admission that he is without official papers leads him to also admit to her that he has a knife. Furthermore he equates it with security and protection that official papers would provide:

> DUMMY The knife is my papers. You must have a weapon when you live on the streets and have no papers. I am a good shop-looter. That is why I have money [...] I steal my clothes from shop. I steal everything of me. Outside and inside. The knife was given me. It is a gift. (*UR*, p. 174)

The dramatic symbolic significance of the knife as a 'gift' takes on a tragic dimension when the Dummy Actor recounts the actual circumstances of the knife being given to him. He explains to Joan that she lives in the 'before'. He continues, 'I live in the after. Nothing is comfortable there. Or normal.' The dialectic of 'before' and 'after' informs and colours the narrative and thematic structure of the play. This is the process in which the past-as-thesis interacts with the future-as-its-antithesis. This interaction is not solely theoretical but existential for the characters of Joan and the Dummy Actor. The traumatic confrontation between the past and the future embodies an alienated space of internalised, psychological fracture. This interiorised rupture epitomises a crucial aspect of a complex and distinctive dialectic at work: the past is intersecting with and informing the present. This effectively creates a phenomenon whereby time is an experience that anticipates and reflects upon itself. The apex of that dialectic process therefore expresses a potentiality of transcendent materiality. In terms of *The Under Room*, the materiality of the knife embodies a dialectical apex and a potent signifier of a politicised materiality. The knife, like the Dummy, is an inanimate object invested with a signified extra-existential value. This is achieved through a fusion of its object-function with the context of the tragic, ethical dilemma in which that object-function is exercised:

> DUMMY I killed. There is a before and after. Before – the army gang came to our houses. They came out of the morning mist. Even that [...] There are many shootings and shouts. I am thirteen [...] They put knife in my hand. They say kill *one*. Choose – so other live. My parents look at me. Not at each other. I wish them to look at each other. To make choice for me. (*UR*, p. 177)

No such help comes and the character goes onto describe how he killed one of his parents although he will not, cannot, name which parent it was:

> I won't tell you that. I am allowed my shame. Without that there is nothing. Love can betray. Shame – you say it – is faithful to the death. (*UR*, p. 178)

The inanimate anonymity of the Dummy takes on a haunting new equivalence to the knife. It too embodies an extra-existential value and significance which the Dummy Actor is able to articulate. The extra-existential significance of the Dummy is a direct and disturbing meta-symbol. At the moment that the knife has entered his parent's body ('I thought the skin would not want to give. It would push back like a stone – twist my hand – throw knife out of it. No.') the young man transmutes into a commodity robbed of his humanity. The human act of violence – even one coerced by the violent threat of others – immediately, simultaneously brings the user of the knife into a dark communion with the object. They become destined to inhabit a shared, shameful inanimate materiality. To say that violence robs its human perpetrators of their humanity is given visible, visceral power in the figure of the faceless Dummy.

At the end of scene 3 the Dummy Actor takes off his shirt and quietly, and alone, carefully puts the shirt onto the Dummy. This begins a sequence in the latter part of scene 4, in which the Dummy Actor first completes the dressing of the Dummy in his jeans and, finally, at the scene's end, places the knife in the pocket of the Dummy's shirt. The young man has sought an impossible, redemptive act of re-entering his own fractured, lost humanity: metaphorically and literally re-dressing his 'after' self, bequeathing it a remembrance of his 'before' humanity.

This re-entering of his past and himself results, in the following scene, with Joan entering the cellar carrying a lighted torch to talk to the sleeping, dressed figure of the Dummy. She has planned that they will escape together from not only the armed forces but also the scheming, amoral Jack, whose sole motivation is the cash nexus and, with it, survival in a brutal world. Significantly, the Dummy Actor speaks in his own indigenous, Eastern European language, having sought to revisit his past. Clearly immersed in a nightmare, Joan is profoundly troubled by his almost ontological separation from her. He is evidently reliving the dual trauma of having killed his mother, under orders from the soldiers, who have then killed his father, and he screams in his sleep. Joan's former compassion and empathy transform into a disturbing anger in which she shouts and accuses him of his moral crime in killing his mother, albeit under traumatic duress:

> JOAN Wake up! Please. Help me! (*Shakes the Dummy violently*) I can't go on like this! I can't go through any more! (*UR*, p. 192)

She then shouts: 'Who are you? I know nothing about you! I have to run out of my house like a criminal!' She then kicks the Dummy along the floor before she shouts at him accusingly:

> JOAN You're warped! Warped! The things you did've warped you! Get up! The people you killed can't! What are you celebrating for? Celebrating? (*UR*, p. 192)

It is as if the knife, or rather the acts of violence that inhabit its object-function, is a kind of destructive virus that contaminates everything it encounters. The victims of the violence virus, on becoming infected, immediately become its perpetrators as well. Joan's former liberal and humanistic goodwill and compassion for the young man and his suffering become compromised. They are corrupted by her encounter with him, the knife and the wider world of state-sanctioned and criminal violence that has permeated like a deadly mould into the foundations of her house and life: the cellar or under room. Significantly it is then, towards the end of scene 5, that she makes physical, material contact with the knife:

> JOAN This is the knife you killed your parent with. The wound hasn't healed in you. You sleep but you don't rest. Your coffin is inside you. You sleep in it [...] I'll give you new life. (*UR*, p. 193)

The dark foreboding that her final sentiment expresses takes on a Euripidean horror in scene 7 of the play. To the extent that Joan imbues the Dummy with new life, it is choreographed into a *danse macabre* articulated by the very violence that has caused its inanimate, alienated condition. Like Agaue, daughter of Cadmus and mother of Pentheus in Euripides' *The Bacchae*, Joan is possessed by a Dionysian frenzy of displaced, orgiastic violence as she knifes and dismembers the Dummy. When Agaue enters, carrying her son's decapitated head in her arms, she does not initially realise the killing of which she has been the prime instrument. Under the hypnotic and darkly transforming influence of Dionysian violence, Agaue cannot (or will not) see that what she carries is the son she and the other women have murdered:

> CADMUS [...] Whose head is that you are holding in your arms?
> AGAUE A lion's – so said the women who hunted it.
> CADMUS Then look straight at it. Come, to look is no great task.
>
> *Agaue looks; and suddenly screams.*
>
> [...]
> AGAUE I see – O gods, what horror! Oh what misery!
> CADMUS Does this appear to you to be a lion's head?
> AGAUE No! I hold Pentheus' head in my accursed hand [...] But who killed him? [...]
> CADMUS It was you, Agaue, and your sisters. You killed him. (Euripides, 1972, p. 238)

The Dummy is, in a complex psycho-dramatic equivalence, a Pentheus to Joan's proto-Agaue. Similarly a savage Eucharistic rite of body, blood and dismemberment is enacted in the under room: her unconscious and ontological site. The prologue to her abandonment of restraint and surrender to the overwhelming urge of violence is characterised by dialogic fragments reminiscent of right-wing tabloid headlines:

> JOAN [...] Immigrants. Aliens. They want to take my house. Take our land. Loot the food from our stores [...] You killed your father and mother. That's easy! It's an offence against nature. It's harder to kill strangers! That's an offence against their community! [...] He's a suicide bomber! (*UR*, pp. 200–1)

She rips and slices the Dummy to pieces and great torn strips of its pre-made interior – rubber and foam – cascade around her like a carnival of terror. She begins to utter fragments of the young man's native language that has only previously been heard in the earlier nightmare sequence:

> Hraxczsvzc! Bratschwig! Wroksccxvs! (*Slashes*) [...] Get rid of the evil! Where is it? (*She searches the strips and rags*) Evil! Wickedness? Where? (*She drops the knife. She sits in the chair. She fiddles with strips hanging from her hands*) ... Where? ... Where? ... Where is the evil? (*UR*, p. 201)

Unlike Agaue, however, Joan's actions have not been sanctioned with punitive, fatalistic authority by the sadistic gods of the Greek pantheon. In symbolic terms that embody and express both the material and metaphorical, the 'under room' of Joan's unconscious has been infiltrated by the all-too-human impact of human, not divine, violence. No *deus ex machina* in the form of the god-man Dionysus has entered her consciousness or erupted from her psyche. The traumatic interloper in Joan's life is Jack, an embodiment and instrument of the human-created violence in the world above and beyond the doors of both her cellar and her former potential. It is those forms and forces of violence, state-authorised and criminalised, that rule her world. 'They'll punish me ... Must hide it ... Hide it. Hide it' (*UR*, p. 202) are Joan's final words as she wanders trance-like from the scene of her crime. For Agaue, the final lines she utters are: 'How could I touch his body with these guilty hands?' then 'What part did Pentheus have, then, in my insanity?' Cadmus, her father and the epitome of patriarchal and paternalistic authority, reiterates her responsibility for her guilt with 'He sinned like you, refusing reverence to a god.' The 'god' whose authority Joan's original behaviour at the start of the play has refused is the authoritarian state machine of morality-as-violence which forbade her to show compassion to those marginalised by its dark *modus operandi*. In Bond's originated use of the term, Joan's 'radical innocence', neonatal and pre-conscious in its origins, had anticipated, expected and sought justice for the young man. Confronted by the viral, terminal power of human violence that she then encounters through him, his knife and Jack's psychotic pragmatism, she herself becomes infected. Deprived of justice by the ideological power systems of human society, Joan's compassion turns upon and against itself like Agaue's love for her son: itself constricted by the psycho-political denial of women's social, political and psycho-sexual autonomy by patriarchy. What I refer to as the virus of violence Bond here translates as corruption:

> To enter drama we need a better understanding of corruption and crime. Corruption comes from the conflict between the imperative to justice and the practical necessity of living in an unjust society. In this conflict the imperative to justice readily becomes the need for injustice. Because the need for injustice is self-conflicting, it turns the need for justice into the lust for revenge. (Bond, 2006, p. 218)

As previously discussed, the sister-selves of Joan and Agaue enact a 'lust for revenge'. This 'lust' does not correspond to the dark, phallocentric fatalistic conviction of women's 'innate' and 'chaotic' desire-as-castration as seen in *The Bacchae*. The two women characters do not destroy the male: a male who is both son and sublimated 'lover-son' because of an intrinsic 'original sin' predicated on and by the female. It is rather that the need for justice is corrupted and reversed into the need or lust for revenge. Bond refers to this complex process of mutation in asserting 'Revenge is the pathology of injustice' (2006, p. 218).

In a poem by Bond called 'The Question' (2008), published in *Plays: 9*, he poses the following question:

> Is the child howling in the city gate and raging with a knife
> The story of our common human fate or of lost hope and wasted
>   human life?
> [...]

Deep deep deep are the questions I must ask
Must I cut off the hand that holds the knife to take the knife
    away? (Bond, 2011, p. 252)

As Joan slowly but with a disturbingly quiet calm climbs the stairs
up and out of the under room, Bond's question posed in the poem
radiates like a dark halo of dying ontological rage around her and the
remains of the Dummy. It is a classic example of Bond employing a
'theatre event' to expose the contradictions between the demands of
radical innocence and those of ideology inscribed through repressive
psychological and physical violence.

In his essay 'Freedom and Drama', published along with *The Under
Room* and the four other plays comprising *Plays: 8*, Bond writes:

> Can radical innocence be irredeemably corrupted, the human
> imperative destroyed? [...] Talk of 'unchanging human nature' is
> part of the frightening stupidity that ideology propagates. The
> problem is that technology magnifies the effects of our diminishing
> inhumanness; the past did not have nuclear weapons and radio that
> reaches further than the voice of God [...] Our culture is haunted by
> gods, zombies, phantoms, hysteria, superstitions, racism, patriotism,
> fanaticisms, zealotry and clinical madness. All our impediments to
> humanness. (Bond, 2006, p. 221)

Which human hand originated the imbuing of the function-value of
a knife into a fetishised means of inflicting violence upon another
human being? If the severing of that hand prior to its first-cause origin, the alpha of human violence, had prevented that violence being
enacted, what of the violent act needed itself to resolve the dark paradox of human violence?

In the penultimate scene of the play, scene 8, which follows the
'murder' of the Dummy, the character of Jack appears again. He
surveys the devastation of the under room and reflects upon its
causes and implications. Jack is an intriguing character who in
some explicit sense embodies the violence of the society in which he
seeks to survive. His narrative and plot function in the play centre
upon his role as a cynically pragmatic 'fixer'. He has witnessed the
Dummy Actor 'shoplooting' in the incident prior to the start of
the play – the act which has catapulted him into Joan's flat and

life. Jack is the means by which the Dummy Actor hopes to escape from arrest and certain execution from the armed forces. There is the hope that in the north of Britain illegal immigrants such as himself can live in relative safety and security. Jack is a 'courier' living on the very border of criminality and society, albeit such terms are in traumatic disarray in the violent world of the play. Joan naively imagines that Jack is a member of a revolutionary group of freedom fighters in opposition to the repressive regime. As he makes it clear to her, however:

> JOAN I'm proud there are still people like you who take this risk.
> JACK I do it for the money. Makes me reliable.
>
> JACK *makes a mock-impatient gesture.* JOAN *gives him a larger envelope.*
>
> JOAN You may check it.
> JACK No need. I'll come back if it's short. (*Warning to the Dummy*) You – ready at a moment's notice. They don't give advance warnins. (*UR*, p. 180)

It is only through cash that Jack is prepared to risk his own safety and secure a false passport and papers for the Dummy to escape to the north. There is an echo in this rationale of Combe's observation to Shakespeare in *Bingo* that 'Everyone listens to money' (*B*, p. 19). The money in question in *The Under Room* is the cash that the Dummy has kept from his 'shoplooting' activities. This has been kept in a metal box in the cellar. It becomes clear that Jack has returned to the cellar after his first appearance there in scene 2 and has stolen the money. When Jack then returns in the following scene to collect the cash essential for the transaction to be completed, he is in a position of power. Joan attempts to explain the situation to Jack, wrongly imagining that reasoned argument can counter his aggressively uncompromising pragmatism:

> JOAN He said he had all the money. He only had the money I gave you. He told me he made money shoplooting. You don't make that much shoplooting. I should've asked to see it. (*UR*, p. 182)

With staggering unawareness of her own disconnection from the harsh environment of their society, she says, 'People like him don't live in the real world.' When Jack responds with, 'Yer promised me dosh', Joan's compromised and naive liberal reading of him and the world is expressed in, 'O god why do there have to be people like you!' Even though she apologises immediately, her naivety is further revealed when she says, 'You try to help. Even if it is for money. You take risks. The people you have to deal with must destroy your faith in human decency' (*UR*, p. 183). Jack makes it unmistakably clear to Joan that unless she can secure the outstanding money from some other source by that evening ''is pass is ashes'. The darker *realpolitik* of the reality facing the characters, and especially Joan and the Dummy, is confirmed when Jack and the Dummy speak after Joan has exited. The Dummy confronts Jack with his knowledge that his erstwhile 'saviour' had returned and stolen the money that would have secured his escape. Joan has gone to try and raise the money. Jack anticipates making money out of her, calculating that she will be forced to work as a prostitute for him as her pimp:

> DUMMY What will you do if she will not do that?
> JACK Grass yer t'the army. Yer wouldn't be the first. I do them a favour – they do me one.
> DUMMY Perhaps the friends of the people you betray will take revenge.
> JACK The sort I betray – I'm their only friend. (*UR*, p. 186)

Nevertheless Jack concludes the scene by telling the Dummy that he will get him over the border but warns him not to push his luck:

> DUMMY You think I am lucky?
> JACK Yeh. It could run out. (*Stands*) Nothin' 'gainst yer personal. Let's keep it like that. (*UR*, p. 186)

When Jack returns therefore after the Dummy has been killed by Joan, he is haunted by a power that he suspects and fears the Dummy has over him: 'Some kid? Some decrepit ol' bastard 'oo stuck his nose in? ... Is that why I come?' As he enters the cellar and acknowledges with world-weary certainty, 'She got 'ere first', Jack goes on to observe with some relief:

> It's a relief yer dead. I can talk t'yer easier. Yer almost got me. Last night I thought I'd chuck it in. Go with yer. Get the pack

a' khaki-shites off me back. Teach yer t'survive. Is that what yer wanted? Needed? (*UR*, p. 202)

Like a latter-day Shakespearean anti-hero, Jack soliloquises on the respect that should be afforded to the dead:

The dead've got their proper place – a grave or where their ash is spent – even the wind or sea – where they belong by right – their 'ome. (*UR*, p. 202)

Finally ruminating on the challenge that the wounded humanity and fractured innocence of the Dummy has confronted him with, 'Must yer die before yer can enter the 'uman race?', his final words before exiting are 'Why?' repeated four times (*UR*, p. 203). He comes upon the knife on the floor, picks it up and goes. This final, iconic gesture encapsulates the contradictory feelings within Jack. The knife in one sense serves as a *memento mori* of a person who, whilst robbed of his humanity, has stirred some glimmer of the possibility of the human in his own life. With dark pathos the knife of course also carries within its invested memory of violence and death a sense of the inevitability of future and further violence. Might it also destroy Jack as it has destroyed the Dummy character and Joan? A dialectical tension is signalled within Jack's taking the knife with him. This is a choice between the apparent inevitability of his – and the human – continuing capacity for violence. The alternative, however utopian in terms of the world of the play, is for Jack to imbue the knife with a new significance. This significance is subtly suggested in the final moment of the play. Jack has gone and the Dummy Actor walks into the debris. Looking down at his own destroyed, alienated self, he half moves a strip aside with his foot. He speaks in a dialogic fragment of his language of birth and which haunted his nightmare revisiting of his killing of his parent: 'Brdriczs ... Brdriczs ... Brdriczs'.

Chair (2000)

Chair was first produced as a radio play on BBC Radio 4 on 7 April 2000 and was directed by Turan Ali. Its first stage production was at the Avignon Festival on 18 July 2006, where it was directed by Alain Françon. In May 2012 it entered the short season of Bond plays at the Lyric Studio Theatre, directed by Bond himself.

As with the other two plays that constitute what Bond called 'The Chair Plays', *Have I None* and *The Under Room*, the play's location is given as 'City 2077'. Again, as with these plays, the environment of the play is a harsh, violent society in which an unnamed but authoritarian regime is in control. Its power is enforced by armed forces that patrol its troubled streets. In *Chair* the cast and setting of the play act as a disturbing microcosm of that wider dystopian reality.

Alice is a woman who lives in a converted block of flats in a bleak inner city. She shares this small basic home with Billy. Although physically he is a grown adult, psychologically, mentally and emotionally he inhabits the persona of a boy. Billy sits with boxes of crayons and draws and colours perpetually and obsessively. These drawings cover the wall of the small living room and have the naive direct quality of a young child's drawing. It is when, through a mistaken act of kindness on Alice's part, their enclosed world is ruptured through an encounter with a Soldier and his prisoner, a frail old woman, that tragedy ensues.

The play opens with Alice looking with regular anxiety out of the window onto the streets below. What she sees is the Soldier at a bus stop escorting an old woman who is his prisoner. It transpires a little later that it is a criminal offence to look from one's window and this is partly what causes Alice's nervousness. There is another factor. She feels she recognises the old woman:

> BILLY Why're you still watching now that you've seen? You've been watching ever so long. (*Draws*) It's only people at a bus stop.
> ALICE I thought I'd seen her somewhere.
> BILLY The prisoner? (*No answer*) Before today?
> ALICE Yes.
> BILLY I could have seen down in the street. (*Draws*) Going somewhere.
> ALICE You'd remember. You've got good eyes.
> BILLY Where did you see her?
> ALICE I don't know. (*C*, p. 112)

The tension is exacerbated when Billy, looking up from his drawing, suddenly says to Alice, 'She looks like you.' Alice's heated response seems disproportionate to Billy's seemingly innocent observation. It reflects her deeper anxiety about a deeper connectedness between herself and the old woman:

> BILLY The prisoner looks like you.
> ALICE She doesn't! – Why d'you say that?
> BILLY Cause it's true. Only she's old. Ever so. I'll draw her like a witch. Will the soldier shoot her with his gun?
> ALICE Don't be silly.
> BILLY He might if he gets fed up waiting for the bus. She's cried a lot. It's washed all her face away but left the dirt. She hasn't cried for a long time.
> ALICE You're talking nonsense.
> BILLY I'm not. I can tell. (*Draws*) Where d'you think you saw her? (*C*, p. 113)

The relationship between Billy and his colourings (emanating from an 'internal', reimagined reality) and the people and events happening in society and the world (located in an 'external' ideologically determined reality) is intriguing and mysterious.

Each episodic scene in the play is titled in terms of 'pictures'. Thus, what is effectively scene 1 is named 'First Picture' in the play. Bond has created a symbiotic relationship not only between Alice and Billy but existentially and even ontologically between Billy's drawings and the events in the world.

Billy becomes angrily frustrated by Alice's refusal to let him leave the flat. He begins to draw a picture of her being eaten by a crocodile, an unwitting, haunting premonition of Alice's fate at the hands and processes of the voracious authoritarian state:

> Your face is all ugly cause you're screaming. You look like the lady in the street. (*Draws*) She's been standing there a long time. If she stands much longer she'll fall down. The soldier should let her sit down. (*C*, p. 114)

Alice is alarmed and frightened that Billy's observation of the woman outside and the soldier will alert the neighbours and community to Billy's existence. Billy responds by fearfully asking, 'They won't take me away will they?', at which Alice reassures him that they won't. Billy urges Alice to go outside and ask the old woman her name. Alice responds that it is illegal to speak to prisoners. The potential if not actual interrelationship between what Billy draws and what happens in the world is further alluded to when he says in the context of Alice asking the woman her name:

> Then when I draw her I'll put a little bubble in her mouth and she says 'My name is – '. But I don't know what to put. The drawing'll be spoilt. (*C*, p. 115)

This complex interface between imagined and actual reality is further developed in the context of Billy urging Alice to take a chair down for the woman or soldier to sit on. When Alice cautiously agrees that she might do so, Billy's response suggests that his drawing can determine the encounter:

> ALICE Perhaps I met her once. If I saw her close to I'd – It'll stay on my mind if I don't know.
> BILLY I'll squiggle all over the paper – squiggle her out. Gone – gone – gone. (*Holds up page*) Look. Now you don't have to go down. (*C*, p. 82)

The relationship between Alice and the old woman is intriguing and in one sense central to the narrative and thematic spine of the play. It is also interesting for the sense in which Bond's delineation of the two characters explores mutual but different constructions of the female.

The old woman, reminiscent in some ways of the old woman in *At the Inland Sea* and *Innocence*, and indeed the unseen character in *Have I None*, epitomises a form of physical vulnerability. This vulnerability is expressed through her demeaning incontinence and the fact she has been robbed of speech. What hasn't yet departed or been snatched away through age or suffering is the desire to communicate. This desire and indeed need for utterance and more crucially communication with another human being is mirrored in Alice.

Alice is an example of the many women in Bond's work, stretching back across his entire output, who are troubled, complex and facing problematic choices. She and they are caught in a tangled, complex web of social, cultural conditions and often forced to exist within harshly oppressive political environments. They are often mothers or, in some of the 'later plays', proto-mothers – as is Alice, and Woman in *Innocence*. These various women are generally of the working class or an undefined underclass of hardship, suffering and conditioned disempowerment. Patsy from *The Fool* is a very good example of such a woman who seeks to resist the oppressions of patriarchy and early capitalist formations of economic organisation and power. The will to resist is clear and expressed and yet their capacity to do so in any sustained, meaningful way is profoundly inhibited by the politicised social and cultural conditions of their existence.

In the subtle and complex dynamics and dramaturgy of the encounter and relationship between Alice and the Prisoner, one sees the coming together of Alice with her possibly lost, possibly estranged mother. The encounter between them in the street presents two women meeting after a – long – period of estrangement and separation. It's not known what has caused the separation. It's possible that the cause is psychological and emotional and that the traumatic meeting between them at the bus stop personifies the dislocation in their relationship. It may also be that the wider, oppressive political and ideological environment has enforced separation upon them. Both factors might and could be directly related.

From this perspective one sees in powerful dramatic terms Alice's past having arrived to confront her in her present. This past is characterised as desolate, damaged and exposed in terms of the old woman's psychological and physical persona. Crucially, it cannot speak to her or at least not through language. They share a common need for engagement, communication and possibly reconciliation.

The old woman bites Alice in the struggle surrounding the chair. The Soldier reports this incident to the authorities, and it transpires that the old woman has later been shot and killed by the Soldier. The Officer arrives to try and ascertain what Alice's intentions were in the incident described, and its possible implications. When Alice is being interviewed by the Officer, the fear and pressure of being in any sense related to the old woman, a prisoner on her way to likely execution, forces Alice to deny any known relationship, 'I didn't know her! I couldn't know anyone in that state if I'd lived with them for the whole of my life! Take your photograph off my table where I eat!' (*C*, p. 135). However, when the Officer tries to disparage and further criminalise the old woman: 'Your cheek is scarred. That is where the prisoner bit you', Alice insists that the prisoner had tried to kiss her. This however exposes Alice once more in the eyes of the authorities to the possibility of a prior, personal relationship. The Officer seeks both to exploit Alice's vulnerability and secure a confession from her:

> OFFICER The soldier has it: (*reads*) yanked her head down and bit her cheek.
> ALICE She tried to kiss me.
> OFFICER Why? – if you were two unknowns.
> ALICE How long had the soldiers had her? Did they? (*C*, p. 103)

In taking the chair down to the street for the Soldier and the old woman, Alice's action and her reaction to a perceived need embodies what Bond defines as the 'Human Imperative'. In the situation that then developed, Alice has sought social engagement in the context of demonstrating helpful concern by offering the Soldier the chair. He is initially, if reservedly, appreciative: 'Considerate. (*Sits*) Civvies'd pinch the body bags off the dead t'do their shopping in' (*C*, p. 84). However, the ideological demands and rules of the army forbid him from fraternising with civilians and he becomes increasingly anxious and aggressive to Alice. The Prisoner begins to urinate and also begins to take an interest in making contact with Alice. The basics of human interaction and the related desire for contact and communication become oppressive and unacceptable pressures for the Soldier. There is a sequence of events in which the Soldier, angrily telling Alice to go and to take her chair with her, is subverted by the Prisoner clinging to the chair and crawling between the struts. Alice responds with compassionate concern for the old woman, whom the Soldier shoves and kicks as he tries to extricate her from the chair. The old woman has no language and can only utter sounds, to which Alice responds with, 'My dear – tell me – please (*The Prisoner grasps the chair struts. Alice tries to fondle the back of her hands*) Put your hand though the bars –' (*C*, p. 88).

The scene continues with almost grotesquely farcical consequences as the Soldier descends into violent panic that his prisoner and the situation are chaotically out of control. In this darkly manic scenario he intermittently attacks the frail, vulnerable old woman whilst Alice pleads with her: 'Forgive me – forgive me – forgive me – I can't help you – I don't know what to –' (*C*, p. 122). The Prisoner leans towards

Alice as if, finally, to speak, but in fact bites her face. The Soldier and his actions are driven and dominated by the ideological demands and constraints placed upon him. This engenders a fear that if the incidents with Alice and the Prisoner become public knowledge, he will be severely punished. In this context his automatic and conditioned response is both to blame Alice and to threaten her:

> (*to Alice*) You did this. Brought the chair. (*Shouts up at the windows*) They ain saw nothing! [...] Anyone say otherwise – yer'll be visit. Not official. Me mates! Own mob [...] Worse 'n an inquiry. They'll skin yer alive 'n put it back on backwards. (*C*, p. 122)

The following scene, 'Third Picture', begins with Billy telling a long story of a drawing he has made to Alice who has returned from the events down in the street. The themes and motifs of the story centre on Mr Dot and a journey that takes him through a tumultuous natural landscape. His intention is to get to the end of the world but, by the story's conclusion, whilst he has survived his journey, the storm has washed out his footprints. Intrinsic to Billy's story is the motif of the journey against seemingly overwhelming odds and dangers. It is a story that has macro and micro connotations. As a meta-narrative of the human journey, it attains a telling perspective of the imperative of journeying and struggling to survive but also to create new forms of humanness. As a metaphor of the lives of Billy and Alice it offers some, ultimately misguided, hope that they might survive the travails of their journey through a social, political and psychological landscape that is dislocated and dangerous.

Alice knows and fears that the consequences of trying to act upon a human imperative or compassion and justice will bring the authorities to their door. She then discloses the narrative of how she came to find Billy as a baby and rescue him in a manner that is reminiscent of two of Bond's earlier plays: *Narrow Road to the Deep North* and its later sister piece *The Bundle*. There are also distant echoes of Brecht's *The Caucasian Chalk Circle*. Alice describes how she had heard a cry from a box left in an empty street save for an unknown woman watching the scene from the shadows:

> ALICE [...] She was waiting to see what happened to you.
> BILLY (*boast*) That was me.

ALICE I went back and took you out of the box. You were wet and cold.

BILLY I'm in a story too like Mr Dot. (*C*, p. 95)

The unknown woman in the shadows, whom we presume was Billy's birth mother, held her hand out and struck Alice, just as the old woman, the Prisoner, whom Alice had sought to help in the present, bites her. Alice explains that she had brought the infant baby Billy home even though she should have handed him in to the authorities. When Billy asks why his mother hadn't handed him in, Alice replies, 'Perhaps she couldn't.' The interweaving of the real, told as a story, and the imagined, drawn as a picture and constituting a parallel reality, is evocative. It reveals once again Bond's deep sense of the materiality of the imagination and the co-existent imagined. Billy seems to instinctively understand the ways in which the real is always (re)imagined in its (re)telling, and that the imagined person or event engendered through radical innocence conveys its own dual-surfaced reality:

BILLY If I drew the doorway – and that: the cartons and black dress – one day she might see the picture – I'll put Billy on it so she'll know. (*C*, p. 129)

Like a contemporary Prospero, Bond employs the character of Billy as a kind of Ariel characterised by a radical innocence and sad pathos: 'We are such things as dreams are made of'.

Billy has to be hidden away as in the 'Fourth Picture' an unnamed female Officer comes to interrogate Alice. The Officer's language and dialogue are characterised by the soulless anonymity and bureaucratic jargon of the postmodern state. At the end of a relentless questioning, the Officer announces that Alice will be held on remand and her home closed and sealed. Perhaps as one final attempt to avert the inevitable – arrest, imprisonment and homelessness with all of the accompanying danger for Billy – Alice tries again to explain to the Officer what had happened: her 'story':

ALICE (*flat*) I brought the chair for the soldier. She thought it was meant for her.

OFFICER She saw pity in you. That's why she kissed you.

ALICE She bit me.

OFFICER ... I don't see how you can say that if you maintain ...

ALICE She'd forgotten what pity was. She wasn't used to it. I was the only person who didn't hit her. She took that for a sign of kindness. It was the kindness that frightened her. She bit me. (*C*, p. 136)

As she is about to leave, the Officer embarks on a long speech in which she reassures Alice that she will recommend a non-custodial supervision order. When Alice asks what will happen to the Soldier, it's clear that he'll share the same terminal fate as the old woman. They will both, separately, be 'processed' at a state facility called PrisCit. She provides Alice with the authorities' official, sanitised view of the value and virtues of this agency:

OFFICER PrisCit is not what it is in the public mind. The department provides a choice. A tablet or an injection in a friendly clinic. Without cost to the individual or any intimate circle or organisation. Cremation is provided and a short ceremony offered. There is a list of approved readings and musical items [...] The official in charge speaks only of the good. The former sadness and bitterness go ... The department also provides a floral tribute. Personalised floral offerings encourage emotional excess and other vulgarities. They draw attention to the few surviving social inequalities. In death democracy – or where! (*C*, p. 137)

Alice sees through the antiseptic, depersonalised vocabulary of state language and simultaneously recognises the gravity of their situation. After the Officer has left, Alice quickly but calmly announces to Billy that she must go, and that he must become independent. Terrified, Billy begins to break his crayons even as Alice tries to explain to him the exigencies of the external, real world: 'Billy, I don't choose things. I have to deal with them as they are. You have to do that now. Then you'll grow up' (*C*, p. 139). She explains to Billy what must happen and gives him instructions. It is clear from a subtext poignant with the pathos of her imminent departure that she intends to commit suicide. Unbeknown to Billy in his naive, infantilised view of the world, Alice's ashes will be sent to him and he will be instructed by her to empty them in the anonymous, alienated location of an inner-city car park. For Alice, as for Bond's Shakespeare, her choice to take her own life is itself a courageous, self-empowering moral action. She chooses her own place and time of departure from this life. In doing so she exposes, in the time it takes to kick a chair away by someone hanging themselves, the nightmarish brutality of a regime that dresses itself in the uniform of soul-destroying conformity. As the Officer had expressed it: 'Each is given a block of marble resin and a thornless rose bush [...] The wardens eat their lunchtime sandwiches there' (*C*, p. 137).

Alice grabs with courage and determination, even as Lear grabbed the spade and began to dig at the wall, this final expression of self-empowerment and life-ownership. She envisages and shares with Billy the aftermath of her ashes being emptied over the car park:

> ALICE In the mornings the cars come back. The wheels will pick up the dust. When they drive off that night it'll be on their wheels. They'll spread it on the streets. All of it. Everywhere over the city [...] Walk away [...] Forget me [...] There'll be no flowers. No music. No speaking [...] Nothing they can get their hands on and say it's theirs [...] I was never here. I was never anywhere. I never was. I was nothing. Not even a piece of dust. (*C*, p. 141)

Alice will become no more and no less than the 'Mr Dot' of Billy's earlier story. Yet in a powerful and moving sense, her choice of suicide is like her taking one of Billy's broken crayons and drawing her own destiny. When Billy says to her, 'I'm afraid. I wish I hadn't broken my crayons', she answers, 'You won't need to draw. You'll have real things.' It is as if the innocent creativity of Bond's Clare in *The Fool* faces the challenge of Darkie's politically astute pragmatism as Alice seeks to guide Billy onward on his journey. Creativity dislocated from the demands of the world represents an infantilised, even dishonest disengagement from reality. It will ultimately alienate and destroy the very creativity that defined it, even as Clare's skills as a writer eventually turned upon him. Alice and Billy live in a repressive society where power is enforced through fear and state-sanctioned violence. That society is as much an asylum as was the madhouse to which Clare is ultimately dispatched in *The Fool*. The worlds of the imagination and the worlds of transformative, progressive, practical action in the world must be reconciled.

We see a broad similarity in the way the 'character-clusters' of Clare/Darkie and Alice/Billy operate. Whereas Clare and Darkie epitomise the unresolved binary dialectics of creative vision in relation to radical political action and change, Alice and Billy embody the tensions between a politicised, adult viewpoint, which challenges the oppressive world in which it exists, and the creative radical innocence necessary to envision a new world and renewed human possibilities. Furthermore, both expressions of irreconcilable radicalism face death at the conclusions of their respective plays.

In the 'Fifth Picture', the penultimate scene of the play, Alice's body is hanging in the opened doorway to the bedroom. Billy is absorbed in his drawings and crayoning and seems oblivious to the figure of his dead carer. Her suicide, intended to liberate him into adulthood and survival in the harsh reality beyond the walls of their flat, seems stillborn. Alice had promised that men would come after her departure, and he waits for them to arrive. He talks to himself as he draws:

> (*Draws*) The lady with the chair's got your face. (*Picks up two drawings. Compares them*) Only hers is a puddle [...] P'raps she was your mother. Might've been. (*C*, p. 111)

With the absurd, farcical humour reminiscent of a scene from Ionesco, he repeatedly brushes against her body as he goes through into the other room, each time expressing a polite 'Scuse me please.' As he grabs his overcoat and scarf, preparing for the men to come and then to leave, he asks himself 'Am I becoming a man?' He then half-sings to himself, 'Why-why-why-why-why –'. It is at this crucial dramatic moment of emerging adult self-awareness and its subsequent questioning of the world that he carries out a small but transformative action. He takes a chair and puts the chair by the body. He then 'adjusts the chair's position. He tilts the body onto the back of the chair so that it takes the weight.' The seed that Alice had planted in his consciousness has not perished:

> BILLY Uncomfortable watching you. (*He sits on the chair facing away from the body*) It's hard. (*C*, p. 111)

He falls asleep having been unable to do so the previous night. As he sleeps, there is the sound of a hammering on the door, which is reminiscent of the same dramatic device being employed in *Have I None*. Who is it that awaits Billy at the other side of the door? Will it be, as in *Have I None*, the paradoxical absence of the human but the presence of another, nightmarish post-human future?

In the sixth and final picture, the stage direction says that 'Billy stands in the morning light'. Billy also has a 'rapt expression' as he journeys through an evocative visual and aural landscape of both the contemporaneous world of the play and our own contemporary inner-city, urban reality. After a day travelling through this land-scape, which has the quality of a hallucinatory dream for this man-boy who has never before ventured beyond home, Billy carefully, and with an almost ritual remembrance of Alice and her final instruc-tions to him, begins to scatter her ashes. At the climactic moment in their shared rite of passage, he hurls the final fistfuls of dust into the air. It is at this moment of his, and Alice's, meta-liberation that the world from which Alice had tried to protect him, then belatedly sought to prepare him for, enacts its summary revenge:

VOICE (*off, calls from edge of car park*) Oi! What y'on?

Billy looks towards the voice. A shot. Billy falls dead next to the carton. The dust floats down on him. (C, p. 112)

Billy has, by the moral necessity of Alice's suicide, been drawn into the world that he has spent all of his previous life trying to control and conjure through his redrawing of it.

This final picture of the dust floating down on him brings a posthumous reunion with Alice. Even as they are finally drawn together in the anonymous materiality of death, they picture a world which, like our own and that of the audience, is facing its own final page.

Before proceeding to the Conclusion and posing the question 'Was anything done?', the following section features an interview with Chris Cooper, Artistic Director of Big Brum Theatre in Education company, in June 2012.

Interview 2
Tell Me a Story: Interview with Chris Cooper

This interview took place in Birmingham in June 2012.

(Peter Billingham) PB   I wonder if we could start by you talking about when you first came into contact with Edward Bond and his writing. How and where did it begin?

(Chris Cooper) CC   It happened in 1988 when I was a young actor in the Duke's Theatre [Lancaster] Theatre in Education company which had been at the forefront of creating an alternative theatre journal about both theory and practice, *Theatre and Education Journal* [*TEJ*]. The director there introduced me to *Lear* and it made a big impact on me. Then in 1991 at the time of the first Gulf War we decided to bring out a special issue of the journal [*TEJ* 4]. I plucked up the courage to write to Edward Bond and ask if he'd contribute a piece to that issue. He responded by writing an essay entitled 'Drama and the Child'. From that point I had intermittent contact with him through being part of the SCYPT committee [The Standing Conference of Young People's Theatre] and he used to make written contributions to the SCYPT conferences. Then eventually Big Brum approached him and said 'you've written in defence of theatre in education, why don't you write a play for us?' That was before I joined the company but that's how he came to write *At the Inland Sea*, his first play for Big Brum. In 1997 he wrote *Eleven Vests* for the company and I was an actor in that production. We re-toured it then later in 1999 by which time I was still an actor in it but also by that time directed it as well.

PB   What was your background in terms of training for theatre?

CC   I went to what was then Newcastle Polytechnic which went on to become the University of Northumbria. I was a student on the Creative and Performing Arts course there from 1983 to 1986. That's where I first discovered my passion and commitment for theatre in education and also first encountered the plays of Edward Bond. I saw a student production of *Tin Can People* in about 1987 but interestingly I didn't really like or understand it – I was quite judgemental about the production, in fact.

PB   At that stage were you aware of and interested in drama practitioners like Dorothy Heathcote?

CC   She and Gavin Bolton were a very big influence because of course both of them taught in the north-east. Geoff Gillham and David Davis trained up there too. I was taught Theatre in Education at Newcastle Polytechnic by Tony Good. The big influences in terms of contemporary drama at that time were writers like Tony Marchant, David Hare and Jim Cartwright. That was where my drama and theatre training and experience started but it wasn't until I came to work in Theatre in Education that I was really inducted into the work of Edward Bond.

PB   What was the initial impact?

CC   I don't think I was very well schooled in theatre although I had been to the theatre a lot. My background was initially working class. I was one of those very lucky people whose parents took them to the theatre a lot. We used to go especially to the Sheffield Crucible or the West Yorkshire Playhouse. I therefore got to see some Shakespeare and some of the other major writers but it also tended to be writers like Alan Ayckbourn. Whilst I enjoyed his work it didn't move me at all and looking back my frame of reference was really quite narrow. My experience of Shakespeare was really based on what I'd studied at school and I thought I hated Shakespeare. I realised eventually that I didn't hate Shakespeare but I did hate the way it was taught. Then later on I came to Bond's *Lear* and I remember being asked if I knew Shakespeare's *King Lear* and I remember saying, well no, I don't. I was a bit embarrassed to admit it because I'd been studying Drama at Newcastle for three years and I didn't know *King Lear*. Then I was invited in that context to read Bond's *Lear* first and I had this profound memory of when the sisters are sticking the knitting needles into the ears of Warrington. I remember being both appalled and delighted at this horrible cruelty. Later in the play when the regime authorises the cutting up and opening of the dead body of one of those sisters – Lear's daughters – he begins to describe the nature of the presence of posthumous beauty in his daughter's body. That moment had such an incredible impact upon me as a young man and that was simply reading it. I knew then that there was an important connection between almost the sheer comic horror and tragedy of Fontanelle and Bodice and their needles. Then suddenly this father sees the beauty of his daughter in an entirely different and unexpected way and the way that the body was used to connect to these incredible ideas. It actually opened up theatre for me in a way that I'd never experienced before. It opened up something very deeply in me as a person. Interestingly it also helped me to read Shakespeare's *King Lear* which I read almost immediately afterwards. I have a most extraordinarily profound memory of the impact of that scene in Bond's play. I can even remember the edition of the play and the pages that were snapping off of the spine. I didn't understand why the play was different from anything I'd read or seen before. I also knew that it was something that I really did need and want to understand more deeply. I then set out to read every play by Edward Bond that I could get my hands on.

PB I also grew up in a working-class family. I remain the only person from my past to enter further and then higher education. When I went to train as a Drama teacher I remember the Head of Drama taking us to see a production of *Saved* at what I think was the Watford Palace Theatre. This was 1972, which was probably the first or second out-of-London tour of the play following its post-abolition of censorship production. What actually stayed with me was the very final scene rather than scene 6 in which the baby is infamously stoned to death. It was that final scene where there's just that one line of dialogue. Len says 'Fetch me 'ammer.' I don't think I fully understood the play. However, it had a very powerful impact upon me. It was tactile like being in the blast of some amazing creative explosion. It's interesting in a sense that we both came to Bond's writing from a broadly shared background. When was the first time you actually directed his work?

CC   1999. That was the second production of *Eleven Vests* which I spoke of earlier. I think you had a certain advantage over me which is that by the time I came to Bond you were already familiar with his writing. It was first of all on the page but it was also after he'd been neglected so actually I didn't see his earlier plays performed until the Lyric last year [2011]. When I did see *Saved*, I thought it's like finding the missing link. It's the critical bit of DNA in understanding the post-war journey of contemporary theatre. I think you can't fully realise Bond's importance until you've seen the work in performance. For me my practical experience of Bond's work had been student productions and then being in *At the Inland Sea* in 1997 before directing it in 1999. I had the benefit of standing on the shoulders of the first production. I'm not sure I would have coped very well with *Eleven Vests* if I'd not had the benefit of Geoff Gillham's guidance as director of the first production. I had that supportive environment if you see what I mean?

PB   Looking back from your perspective as a younger actor was there a particular kind of challenge coming to this very distinctive and powerful writing? The fusion of art and politics, did that pose a challenge?

CC   I think it challenged absolutely everything that I thought I knew about acting. The nature of my training at Newcastle hadn't been very technical anyway and the kind of theory that we paid attention to tended to be more political or pedagogical rather than dramatic. I mean we did talk about Brecht and we did talk about Stanislavsky but I never really understood about how to perform Brecht. There was this underlying and simplistic assumption, from me at least, that Stanislavsky was somehow 'bad' and Brecht implicitly 'good'! I brought all of that baggage to performing Bond. I realised in the doing of it that I'd been relying as an actor up until that point on a kind of fairly basic Stanislavskian approach. A heightened and activated 'emotionalism' drove me through everything. It was a terrible shock. I experienced creative paralysis for the first time in my life but Geoff thankfully was very good at helping and understanding. Both he and everyone who had been in the original production of *At the Inland Sea* had learned so much. This changed the way from then on about how everyone thought about theatre and acting. Geoff was very strict as a director for very good reasons and so he wouldn't let me get away with what I'd been doing as an actor up until then. Talk about the 'blank canvas!' There were times when I thought I just can't do anything because I can't 'situate myself in the problem'. I was trying to short-cut the process with emotion and 'generalising' as an actor and realising that you can't 'short cut' Bond's writing. Furthermore you can't engage either in a sort of Brechtian 'commentary' upon it. I'll never forget that experience. The first production of *Eleven Vests* was full of that kind of 'comment' and mostly from me. I was play- ing it 'in my head'. I recognised that I wasn't letting the play speak through me because I didn't know how to. I think that's stayed with me as a director and I can recognise when that problem is happening for other actors and hopefully I can help them. For me at the time, you felt as if you couldn't breathe properly, you couldn't use your hands. Normally before that I'd just 'do stuff' as an actor but I realised that I couldn't and shouldn't do that anymore. The text won't let me do that and the director was being very good because he won't let me do it either. So, I have to understand the play, the writing and what it demands of me.

I had real integrity but it was as if I was putting a lot of creative sweat into doing and achieving nothing. It just couldn't work.

PB   Were there any particular ways that Geoff had of working on the script that you found helpful?

CC   I have a very strong memory as an actor of Geoff offering an image of working in a department store. He said if you know what an old-fashioned department store was like – the text can move you from one department in the store to another instantly – like that. You don't have to go through a psychological or naturalistic proc- ess to get there. The 'departments' are like signposts and that's how the mind works. At first it felt very strange because it feels ever so slightly psychotic. Then I realised how close that was to the idea and feeling of 'being in the moment'. Therefore you experience feel- ing that isn't necessarily connected to the previous feeling. It's not that it's random – there's a structure to your experience – but you become capable of moving from extreme to extreme. From 'lingerie' to 'delicatessen' instantly so to speak!

PB   That really resonates with what Edward Bond has to say about actors not playing characters but playing environments. It sounds as if that was Geoff's way of utilising and communicating that idea for actors. When you're in that environment, in that location and on that site, there's a kind of encounter?

CC   That's absolutely right and it's the particularity of it that's so liberating and helpful. Geoff's thinking was driven by working with Edward Bond. Then in 1999 with the second production of *Eleven Vests*, Edward Bond was drafting *The Hidden Plot*. He was sending us the essays in process as we were rehearsing. I think at that time I was still tending to make those ideas too abstract in rehearsal although I've since learned my lesson. Understanding how the 'dramatic site' works at such a social and psychological level is remarkable and incredibly concrete. If you say, for example, that you're at the point where the enemy is about to be stabbed with the bayonet for the second time, it's not enough. Fear is not just fear. It's a particular fear in a particular moment on a specific site. You express your fear in a particular way. If you get me to encounter a policeman I express my fear of their authority in a very different way from the way that I would if I was in fear of you. You can find yourself then responding in some remarkable ways. They're always helpful providing that they're 'situated'.

PB   Any attempt to generalise or 'act' a response and the writing and its meaning will evade you?

CC   We really struggled with that in *Have I None* because that was my first production of really standing on my own two feet as a director and this play was such a radical shift again from anything I'd ever done. How you open the door when there is the knocking offstage? The actor playing Sara who hears the knocking on the door and must open it experiences a fear. How do you play that fear? Edward was working with us in rehearsals and was just hammering home and being extremely perceptive. There are the notes and the essays of course but when he's there in the rehearsal room working with you he's there, absolutely there. His ideas are like the theoretical scaffolding but what he absolutely understands is that the play, in practice, must 'tell itself'. We need to know how to use the play in performance.

PB   In that play [*Have I None*] there are moments when it seems as if 'Edward Bond meets Ionesco, meets Feydeau'. There are of course farcical moments interwoven with others of dark psychological and emotional power. Consequently there is this incredible coming together and clash of apparently disparate elements.

CC   He often talks about 'washing lines' and what's hung on the washing line and how it's taken down. He talks about the particularity of the social through the individual in any given historical moment. I remember him saying to me in a rehearsal of *Have I None* 'Where have the knocks gone, Chris?' Then you begin to revisit the moments in the play when the knocks occur and who appears and enters after them? It made me think about the play and its site in a completely different way. 'Where have the knocks gone?' Well they've moved into a sneeze or a scratch or a woman with an obsession about a painting in a ruined house. You suddenly then realise that the question is absolutely concrete and not theoretical.

PB   It's as if the play itself and the characters in that dramatic location are themselves 'the knock'? I felt this when I watched the Lyric production. The characters onstage are themselves on a site that is a kind of 'outside'. They are on an 'outside' dimension of another 'inside' site. There's that powerful moment when Sara enters in that amazing costume? It's in scene 3 and the stage direction describes Sara's costume as 'She wears a ground-length loose coat of stiff sky-blue silk. It is covered with metal spoons. They are stitched to the silk so they cannot swing loosely but can knock against each other when the coat moves.'

CC   When I first read that I thought what is that about? This is unreasonable. I don't understand this and I'm not sure that I ever quite did. What I did experience was extraordinary response from the young people to it. It was almost personal. I know I learnt a lot about the play and its meanings through working with the young people who watched it and shared their ideas after the performance. Now I'd approach it quite differently. In 2010 Edward and I saw a triple bill of *Have I None*, *Chair* and *People*. In scene 3, where she is intended to enter in that costume, in the triple-bill production she simply entered in a blue cape. When we asked the director afterwards 'Why did you do that?' he simply answered 'Oh, it's because it [the original costume] doesn't work.' It reminded me of how I'd used to generalise as an actor all of those years before. In doing so, you try and step over the problem rather than confront it. There was a similar problem that the director had in their production of *Chair*. You have to deal with and face the problem of the old lady climbing into the chair [in scene 2, referred to as 'Second Picture']. They just cut the whole sequence and what you miss is the site and the centre of the play. In *Have I None* the 'knock' is 'knocking loudest' at that point. What that director was really saying was 'I don't understand this' and so he just got rid of it.

PB   Has there been a particular play of Edward's that has had a special value and meaning for you? It's a kind of *Desert Islands Disc* question [*Laughter*]. If you could only take one of Edward Bond's plays with you to the island, which one would it be?

CC   I'm not sure I actually have an answer. Every play that Edward has written for us and continues to write for us takes us to the very edge of our creative competency. It always takes me and all of us to the limits of our understanding. I always feel quite obsessed with the play that I'm working on at the particular time. That becomes *the* play and I'm very bad at stepping back and making a more objective, comparative judgement. Like at the moment we're doing *The Broken Bowl* and I think it's a wonderful play and the best so far. I'll be doing *The Edge* in the autumn and *that* then will be the 'best'. They all make real challenges to both me and the company. We learn about them and make discoveries as they go out 'on the road' too. Next week we're going to have an additional day's rehearsal on *The Broken Bowl* even though it's been touring schools for two months already. There's still much to develop. I remember the first time I read *The Balancing Act* I put it under my bed for a week and thought I'm not looking at this (Figure 5). When I first read *The Under Room* I thought this was a brilliant play. I also mistakenly in retrospect thought 'I understand it!' I saw the character of the Dummy Actor and thought immediately, ah yes, this is quite like a Brechtian device. I then realised through beginning to work on the play that I was mistaken and that it was something more layered and textured.

PB   There's been this long-standing misconception for a long time about the seeming connections between Brecht's and Bond's writing.

CC   The company also thought the same the first time they read it together with me. I said to them, no, it's not, but don't worry – I've already faced that crisis for you!

Figure 5 Liz Brown as Viv in the re-toured production of *The Balancing Act* by Big Brum, directed by Chris Cooper. In a darkly farcical way the character of Viv, seen here with the blanket that she constantly clutches, lives in a derelict house in which she believes there is a spot or place in the room which 'Keeps the world in balance. If it was trod on the balance'd go. The world'd spin. Fast. Everythin spin off in t'space. People'd be pull out a' their 'ouses' (Bond, 2011, p. 112). Her nightmare vision of the precarious existential and political condition of the world is ultimately proven true in the final scene of the play.

There is always something challenging and stimulating in every one of the plays. What you rightly called the 'collision' of genres in *Have I None* was such a departure from *At the Inland Sea* and *Eleven Vests*. That was the newness in it that really challenged me and which I loved in a 'perverse' sort of way. I also 'hated' it in that initially I didn't know how to deal with it.

PB   Are there other examples in your experience?

CC   I've already referred to the Dummy Actor and the Dummy in *The Under Room*, a tremendous challenge but great to work on. Then *Tune*, which you saw of course, the sheer joy of working on that with nine-year-old children. It was simply audacious. Seeing the way that the children responded to it at nine makes you feel as an adult completely inadequate. I'm not answering your question am I?

PB   It was more my thinking whether working on particular plays had a special remembrance for you? The demands that they make upon all of us directors who've worked on them are indeed considerable. Sometimes we think we've made some partial discoveries and found some provisional answers to the questions they pose for us, the actors and the audience.

CC   All of the 'eureka' moments have happened for me when we finally put the work in front of young children and than I think – ah, yes, that's what it means. I'm supposed to be 'the expert' when it comes to working with young people. However, I think Edward understands them better in a very different kind of way. If I had one real epiphany it was the first time we did *The Window* and the woman has committed suicide; she leaves the room while her son is asleep and there's a loud crash as she hangs herself. He wakes up and there's music playing. The son begins to clear up the mess his mother has made in the room. As he does so he dances to the music and cries. It's very powerful. Very strange. The first time that Danny [the actor playing the son] was in performance we hadn't had time to work on it at all. He just did it and when he'd finished the room was just … I couldn't speak. We were sat in stunned silence. It was then, as you said earlier, 'it's all there in the play'. I was reminded of what dramatisation is and the power of enactment. Danny had felt he didn't know what his character was doing but in fact he understood the site. As an actor he was dealing intuitively and with great discipline with the problem of dancing and crying but not knowing what he was crying. I was on the edge of tears as was everyone in the rehearsal room but I managed to say, 'We've just experienced accident time' and I really understood accident time. The actor can never have that first time again. But accident time is not for the actor, it's for the audience. Danny had demonstrated a remarkable capacity to step into the site and be enactive. We had another two weeks of rehearsal to go and we knew we couldn't experience that incredible moment again. I realised however that this was what the young audience experienced every time – because it was the first time for them too. The power and energy of that moment of dancing and crying must be extraordinary for the young people who, in each performance, are confronted by that powerful image.

PB   I had a similar experience with a young actress in *The Children* who had a line 'It hurts' after the ritual bonding stoning of the dummy. It was as if a bird had flown out of a net that it had been caught in. This young actress just spontaneously took and cradled the broken dummy. It could have been an image out of a Renaissance painting of Mary cradling the dead Christ from the cross. She looked at it and in that moment existentially, experientially *knew* that the 'hurt' of the inanimate dummy was simultaneously her own wound as one of the perpetrators. It was about two or three days later before I could talk with her about it and say, 'So what do you think happened in that moment?' It confirmed for me that if we simply encounter the work and let it meet with and encounter us, let it speak to us, can speak far more than any amount of theoretical writing about the plays. There is something that is so physical, visceral and sensual about the work.

CC   I agree so much with what you're saying. It's interesting what you've said about theory somehow getting in the way of actually meeting with and working on the plays themselves. The lesson I've learned is that we have to work with the plays, really work with them and allow them to confront us as they do with our humanness. There is a strong dialectical relationship of about what is written about the work and its realisation in practice. However, I think that if you allow what's written about the work to come between you and your work on the play then you're really scuppered. The theoretical writing is as I mentioned earlier like the scaffolding. It helps to give you a sense of structure in which to work but it should never come between the play and one's direct working upon it. As Edward Bond said, drama is about the relationship between the edge of the universe and the edge of the kitchen table. You'll only ever find the universe if you know how to use the cup on the table to drink tea.

PB   You get that powerful sense of both the functionality of objects and their metaphorical meaning.

CC   Absolutely. What's been the favourite thing in all of the plays have been the objects and that's the teacher as well as the artist in me speaking. In *The Broken Bowl* the bowl always retains its 'use value' but it also has not only a metaphorical but a metonymical value and that's extraordinary. When the father breaks the bowl and thinks he's solved the problem, the sound of that bowl breaking is as if he's caved his daughter's skull in, which of course, in a metonymic sense, is precisely what he's done.

PB   Thanks so much, Chris.

CC   Thanks, Peter.

Conclusion: 'Was Anything Done?'

'Was anything done?' is the last line uttered by Shakespeare in Edward Bond's *Bingo* and seems an appropriate and intriguing title for this short Conclusion. From the same play, shortly after the Old Man has been shot and killed offstage, Shakespeare reflects with a bleakly austere truth:

> Every writer writes in other men's blood. The trivial and the real. There's nothing else to write in. But only a god or a devil can write in other men's blood and not ask why they spilt it and what it cost [...] Was anything done? Was anything done? (*B*, p. 57)

In an ideological environment characterised as 'post-dramatic', drama has effectively been afforded the last rites. The intention has been that it should be interred and share similar obituaries with both the author (Barthes) and history itself (Fukuyama). From this perspective, the possibility and relevance of political drama have come under increasingly dismissive scrutiny from such postmodern critics in the past two decades.

In 'Six Little Essays', which Bond wrote for the programme of the six-play season at the Cock Tavern Theatre in 2010, he attacked this thinking as 'post-mortem' rather than 'post-modern':

> We have no political theatre. Yet politics is at the heart of self and society. Drama deals with the relation between self and society. Each creates the other. That is how we create our humanness. Political drama must look at the profoundest human paradoxes.

Greek drama did this for us. All Western culture and religion have been founded on this inheritance [...] We have exhausted it. Our dramas – our culture, our politics – are dead. Post-mortem not post-modern. If we do not create a new drama that looks at the profoundest human paradoxes we will destroy ourselves.

In an interview with this author, Bond observed:

Marx is absolutely true in saying that history is a product of our material relationship to the universe but I also think that imagination is material and I think it's false to make that distinction or division. It's just an ideological contrivance. Marx is right about this but he doesn't sufficiently explain how this happens. (Billingham, 2007, p. 5)

Bond's assertion earlier in his career that 'All imagination is political' (1987, p. 5), resonates in his reference in this interview to 'imagination is material'. The focus upon 'humanness' is revealing. It illustrates an extended development of his earliest humanist materialism into even deeper philosophical and ethical territory. This might be identified (though not exclusively) as starting from the mid 1990s onwards. That period was clearly crucial in terms of Bond's work. It was from the mid 1990s onwards that his pre-existing reputation in Britain and beyond became enhanced in a new, high-profile international context. Through Alain Françon, especially, Bond arguably entered a major new phase in his writing, its production and critical reception. After a period of effective exile from Britain, the plays which constituted 'The Paris Pentad' opened important new creative opportunities for Bond. This was also, as previously identified, the beginning of what has remained an incredibly fruitful relationship with Big Brum. The deepening development of Bond's wider critical and theoretical thinking was both a consequence and contributor to this new-found recognition and opportunity for his plays. I believe it brought with it an increasing interest for Bond in the ontological and with it the associated concerns of being, consciousness and knowing. Within this tri-dialectic Bond developed a strong engagement with Kant, especially his *Critique of Pure Reason* (1781):

In his philosophical writings Kant is saying [...] How is it possible to know anything, as a response to Hume. What this however then introduces is the question of 'What is value?' What he [Kant] is saying is there are two things that are really incompatible but it is so and they are both true. The world is Newtonian in that we are objects in a machine that is the universe. However, he also says that we have a moral sense and that doesn't make any sense because where does it come from? The Enlightenment doesn't seem able to provide an answer. (Billingham, 2007, p. 9)

For Bond, the human motivation to create drama has become increasingly viewed as located predominantly beyond the social, cultural and ideological boundaries of its normative Marxist cultural-materialist usage. Some critics have argued that this development in his thinking has run the risk of accommodating a neo-spirituality problematically close to Hegel's 'World Spirit'. This is a philosophical concept that, unsurprisingly, Bond has consistently opposed and attacked. In addition to the relative failure and ultimate collapse of Soviet state communism in 1989, Bond sees a problematic connection between the allegedly irresistible power of 'World Spirit' and the 'historical inevitability' of the dictatorship of the proletariat in Marxist ideology. As young men, like many other contemporary German radicals, Marx and Engels had started their radical endeavours as 'Young Hegelians'. It is arguable that Prussian nationalism and Stalinist totalitarianism respectively were both ideologically subsidised by Hegelian and Marx–Engels dialectical inevitability.

When Bond talks or writes of drama as existing upon a site and having an ontological foundation and function, he is not in my view proposing either a narrowly essentialist or existential metaphysics of being. Mark Ravenhill, a great admirer of Bond's writing, offers the following observation in an article about Bond that he wrote for *The Guardian* on 9 September 2006:

Bond's political philosophy is a personal form of humanist Marxism. But while at some stages in his writing career Brecht attempted to write to the party line, Bond's is a more idiosyncratic vision. In many ways it's a very English sensibility. There's [...] anger about the way goodness is corrupted by the brutalisation and bureaucracy of society, that are close to Blake or the Shelley of *The Mask of Anarchy*. (Ravenhill, 2006, p. 4)

Ravenhill recognises a 'very English sensibility' in Bond's dramatic vision. He also appropriately identifies a small but significant link in the political-historical 'DNA chain' of radical English nonconformity between Bond and Blake and Shelley. Bond asserts in an article:

> What is drama's purpose? The human mind is a dramatising structure. We have only one way of creating humanness: drama. Boulevard theatre glosses over the human paradox. Performance art thinks the solution is transcendental. Beckett thinks there is no solution. Brecht thinks that if a problem is clearly shown the solution can be found by thought. If that were so there would never have been a need or use for ideology. Euripides said you cannot talk reason to the mad – the clinically or socially mad. Drama deals with the human paradox. It uses situations – often extreme – in which the contradictions become critical. (Bond, 2004, n.p.)

Bond's methodological concept of 'theatre events' should not be confused with the 'shock tactics' of what Bond in the earlier years of his writing called 'aggro-effects'. These included, infamously, the calculated blinding of Warrington in Bond's radical deconstruction of Shakespeare's tragedy in his 1971 play:

> Theatre Events reveals the hidden site [...] The audience are shown their site by being placed in it – not, as in Brecht, outside it. Accident time replaces alienation effect. In the site the audience is faced with the human paradox. A paradox cannot be 'taught'. Nor may its solution. There is no solution to the problem of being human. A paradox may only be shown. Faced with it we create our humanness or destroy our humanness. (Bond, 2000b, p. 48)

Bond develops the use of the 'theatre event' in an exemplary way in *Lear*, as explained in the following extract from his interview with Ulrich Koppen. Koppen asked Bond about his specific implementation of the 'theatre event', to which Bond's answer is revealing:

> Koppen: How does your concept of TEs differ from that of other dramatists' understanding – say Shakespeare's – of comparable theatrical notions?
> Bond: I add to the concept of TE the concept of use [...] The TE uses an incident in a play in an entirely different way to

what you might expect. In the scene of Gloucester's blinding in Shakespeare's *King Lear*, for example, he uses a seventeenth-century TE, but in my *Lear* I put in a modern TE. In Shakespeare's TE the servants attend the blinded Gloucester. In my TE the servants first attend their dead fellow while Gloucester crawls about the stage. They are different TEs. All stories are usable in that way. (Koppen, 1997, p. 104)

Bond's output as a dramatist demonstrates an ongoing evolution of ideological discourse and post-structural innovation. The defining characteristics of his theatre emerge out of a compelling interplay of heightened, textured, dramatic language and the impact of his evolving vocabulary of critical thinking. From 'aggro-effects' through to the 'Internal Transcendent' these way-marks reveal an unremittingly forensic commitment to articulating a new form of political drama. These are exemplified through such previously cited examples from *Lear* and the infamous iconic status afforded the stoning of the baby in *Saved*. This interplay is always towards a political end, although not in any narrow, sectarian sense. Bond's political position and perspective I believe rest upon a deeper concern for what it means to be human and how a more just and equal human society can be built. In keeping with the transformative insights expressed through Bond's key concepts such as 'radical innocence', it is a revolutionising of human consciousness itself that is required. This radical process goes beyond the polemic, didactic 'consciousness raising' of earlier twentieth-century stages in the dialectic of Marxist and socialist theory and activism. This is one important factor why, for Bond, the strategies of Brecht's Epic Theatre and the alienation effect have become, arguably, not only problematic but actively redundant. His ultimate and savagely uncompromising ethical judgement on Brecht should dispel any residual conviction that the mature Bond of his late-middle and later period has any meaningful relationship or affinity with Brecht.

An epilogue: 'The sound of the human voice will comfort us'

In the 'later plays' Edward Bond revisits major themes from his early and mid-career whilst also entering into a deepening concern with philosophical issues, especially his exploration of the ontological strata in human existence.

It is pertinent at this point to refer to a respected critic and scholar writing about Bond's plays in his early to mid career. The following quote is taken from Simon Trussler:

> Unlike, say, Beckett, who has left critics to work out their own interpretations of his ambiguities, Bond has clearly indicated by way of preface and interview what his plays are 'about' [...] Bond writes about man in his environment – and man has made that environment an unnatural one, whether in the South London streets of *Saved* or the mythic kingdom of *Lear*. Bond chooses elemental subjects – violence, pity, aggression, love, greed, fear – but conceives them in minutely particular and human terms. (Trussler, 1976, pp. 33–4)

That observation by Trussler of the almost forensic degree of close, analytical observation and painstaking craft reminds one of what William Blake referred to as 'the holiness of the minute particular'. It is to see 'a world in a grain of sand, / And a heaven in a wild flower' (Blake, 1971, pp. 741, 585).

It is arguable that Bond might be seen to share, if only in a latent and symbolic sense, Blake's radical and revolutionary vision within a history of English, and especially working-class, nonconformism. Bond also epitomises the insistently provocative political and ethic ferocity of Blake's 'Tyger', pacing the burnt-out shopping arcades and desolate lives of the contemporary inner city.

To the extent that there are or might be 'answers' to the 'questions' posed in early plays like *The Pope's Wedding* and *Saved* and in the 'later plays' from *The Children* onwards, they are at best provisional. In some important respects, Bond appears to have returned to those original questions. In revisiting them, his creative process constitutes the excavation of new, deeper levels of humanness in order to try and make some new discovery or insight which would help us learn to 'sing in the ruins'.

The question of the continuing impact of human violence upon our society, culture and political systems has neither abated in the wider world nor as a centrifugal force in Bond's writing.

In an iconic and provocative article by Terry Eagleton from 1984, he analyses very interestingly Bond's use of terms such as 'nature' and 'culture'. Eagleton frames his discussion that he is in 'political solidarity with Bond's aims'. He also acknowledges and affirms the extensive amount of commentary and analysis that Bond has produced about his own work. Whilst it is clear that Bond has disassociated his thinking and plays from Freud, I have some sympathy with Eagleton, who observes:

> One can imagine the scorn he would pour upon Freud, as a bourgeois ideologue out to 'fix' human nature beyond all social determination [...] Sexuality for Freud is not a 'need' but a 'drive' [...] The continuity between our infantile needs and adult politics which Bond wishes to underline occurs only in the context of the most unsettling discontinuity we are ever likely to experience – the break precisely, from nature to culture, need to desire, of which the Oedipus is effective sign. (Eagleton, 1984, pp. 131–2)

It is possible and reasonable to view some of the character relationship–dynamics from a carefully nuanced proto-Freudian perspective. I believe that, if taken conditionally and with care as metaphors of the presence of desire and its implications in human consciousness, motifs such as the 'Oedipal complex' are safe enough to swim around. Nevertheless I also retain a critical and uneasy awareness of the complex, patriarchal, class and gender determinants of *fin-de-siècle* Vienna in which Freud established his principal theoretical models. I do not of course assert some crude, reductive 'influence' of Freud upon Bond's theoretical and dramatic intentions. Nevertheless there is evidence to suggest that a psycho-dramatic reading of character relationships such as Fontanelle and Bodice with Lear, and Joe's relationship to his mother and the 'Dark Man', might yield some insights.

I conclude this book with a short extract taken from a poem written by Bond called 'Torturer's Lament', which is published alongside his play *The Woman* in *Plays: 3*. It ensconces for me a biting metaphor of not only the potentiality but also the degradation of human culture and especially drama. Simultaneously it also evokes the bleak emptiness and nihilism of human existence denied humanity and denied hope:

Then you hear on the news
The investigation has to stop

They take away the one chance you get to relax
The one bright spot in your mind
Is it decent?

You go into that little room
Dark like the pictures
That's where the action is
A chance to be your own boss
Use your imagination
Watch someone else crawl for a change. (Bond, 1987, pp. 282–3)

Whilst of course the 'little room / Dark like the pictures' is, in a literal sense, the interrogation and torture chamber, the image also evokes associations of the theatre as a building and a cultural artefact. Within so much of contemporary reality TV, tabloid culture and mainstream, ultra-commercial populist theatre, the dark little room is a place where a cocktail of voyeurism and instant gratification projects its distortions onto the screen of social, cultural and even political life.

Echoing metaphorically the subversive political strategies of 'The Situationists' (a revolutionary organisation active in the 1960s), Bond seeks to 'disrupt the spectacle' and smash the screen of reactionary, authoritarian homogeneity. In endeavouring to 'disrupt the spectacle' of early twenty-first-century socio-economic, cultural and ultimately political reality, Bond's 'later plays' have I believe excavated new and deeper strata of dramatic realities and a further awareness of human imagination as the dramatic site.

These plays, and others from this period not discussed within this book, not only reflect back upon Bond's lifelong journey as a writer but also define a new dramatic and political territory for his work. The anger at injustice and the oppressive nature of totalitarian regimes and the ideologies that inform them has not abated. The unsentimental but dramatically crafted compassion for the poor and marginalised remains. Nevertheless what does emerge in these plays, and I would date this back to and include plays such as *At the Inland Sea*, is a deepening complexity and layering of the texturing of materiality. This may be seen in the following short extract from the Old Woman's speech in that play. She lifts her smock to reveal a filthy, bloody dress beneath. Like a Euripidean guide escorting the

Boy through a Breugel-esque landscape of suffering she speaks to the Boy:

> This is nothing? I walk among dead and dying! [...] Look! (*Points to a stain*) – tears from an old mother mourning her butchered grandchildren. Here's a woman driven mad with suffering – she ripped it with her teeth. This is chips of flesh from a slaughter pit. [...]
> I see more pain in the cracked face of a doll than you see in your baby. I'm wise in pain and sin! (*AIS*, p. 26)

Directly related to this is Bond's ceaseless, scrupulous, ploughing of the furrow of human imagination – its nature and its dramatic and political significance.

I would like to suggest that Edward Bond has in effect offered up a mirror to the times in which he and we live. This is not however from my viewpoint a metaphor or image of what might be seen as his works offering essentially a passive, reactive reflection of the world. It is my view that this misunderstanding would effectively represent the diametrical opposite of what I understand to be Bond's intentions and dramatic strategies. I would suggest that in darkly, powerfully iconic moments in Bond's writing such as Lear's traumatic and cathartic re-envisioning of himself through the mirror-fragment, the slowly swinging body of Alice and the burnt, blackened baby of *Innocence* and *At the Inland Sea*, we see a writer who gazes with unyielding and unflinching courage and unique creative vision upon himself and the world. Was anything done?

Edward Bond was born into a world of imminent terror and destruction and experienced the traumas of both evacuation and a London and Europe devastated by the indiscriminate bombing of civilians and the innocent. This sense of a nightmare world characterised by violence and despair was also perhaps traumatically reinforced by his experience of national service and the brutalising regime of institutionalised army life. It is possible that Bond's experience of a war-ravaged childhood and of post-war, Cold War threat and alienation left a deep and indelible mark upon him, a wound perhaps as deep as the cathartic thrust of Lear's fractured self-knowing and realisation. As fracturing as Joe's complex relationship with his displaced alter ego and other-self: the puppet.

Was anything done? That profound, searching, interrogative question has been articulated by Bond through a long, long journey of writing plays that stand above the cultural, political landscape of our last troubled century and the impending catastrophe of the early millennium.

Was anything done? That question is for us as much as for Bond's Shakespeare and indeed I would suggest for Bond himself. There is a shared responsibility for us all to consider – and collectively, imperfectly and with the vulnerability of our humanness – to seek a provisional answer. It is my view that Edward Bond has and continues to develop and express a fiercely illuminating searchlight upon us and our world – and the possibility of us and it having a future.

Was anything done? I will leave almost the final words to Bond himself:

> My understanding of my own plays has to be limited but I think the immanent transcendent is the dummy in the chair. It is the rock the audience questions. (2012a, xiii)

Who shall cast that first stone – and at what and at whom?

Bibliography

Abel-Hirsch, N. (2001) *Ideas in Psychoanalysis: Eros* (Cambridge: Icon Books).

Billingham, Peter (2007) Interview with Edward Bond: 'Drama and the Human: Reflections at the Start of a Millennium', *PAJ: A Journal of Performance and Art* (*PAJ* 87), 29:3 (September), 1–14.

Billington, M. (2007) *State of the Nation: British Theatre since 1945* (London: Methuen).

—— (2008) Interview with Edward Bond: 'If You're Going to Despair, Stop Writing', *The Guardian*, 3 January, www.guardian.co.uk/stage/2008/jan/03/theatre.

Blake, William (1971) *The Poems of William Blake*, ed. W. H. Stevenson (London: Longman).

Bond, Edward (1977) *Plays: 1* (*Saved, Early Morning, The Pope's Wedding*) (London: Methuen Drama).

—— (1978) *Plays: 2* (*Lear, The Sea, Narrow Road to the Deep North, Black Mass, Passion*) (London: Methuen Drama).

—— (1983) *Lear*, with notes and commentary by Patricia Hern (London: Methuen Student Edition).

—— (1987) *Plays: 3* (*Bingo, The Fool, The Woman, Stone*) (London: Methuen Drama).

—— (1992) *Plays: 4* (*The Worlds, The Activist Papers, Restoration, Summer*) (London: Methuen Drama).

—— (1994–2000) *Letters*, 5 vols, ed. I. Stuart (Chur, Switzerland and Philadelphia: Harwood Academic).

—— (1996) *Plays: 5* (*Human Cannon, The Bundle, Jackets, In the Company of Men*) (London: Methuen Drama).

—— (1997a) *At the Inland Sea: A Play for Young People*, with notes and commentary by T. Coult (London: Methuen).

—— (1997b) *Eleven Vests* and *Tuesday* (London: Methuen).

—— (1998) *Plays: 6* (*The War Plays: Red Black and Ignorant, The Tin Can People, Great Peace; Choruses from After the Assassinations*) (London: Methuen Drama).

—— (2000a) *The Children* and *Have I None* (London: Methuen Drama).

—— (2000b) *The Hidden Plot: Notes on Theatre and the State* (London: Methuen Drama).

—— (2000c) *Selections from the Notebooks of Edward Bond*, vol. 1: *1959–1980*, ed. I. Stuart (London: Methuen).

—— (2001) *Selections from the Notebooks of Edward Bond*, vol. 2: *1980–1995*, ed. I. Stuart (London: Methuen).

—— (2003) *Plays: 7* (*Olly's Prison, Coffee, The Crime of the Twenty-First Century, The Swing, Derek, Fables and Stories*) (London: Methuen Drama).

—— (2004) 'Modern Drama and the Invisible Object', *Journal for Drama in Education*, 20:2.

—— (2006) *Plays: 8 (Born, People, Chair, Existence, The Under Room)* (London: Methuen Drama).

—— (2011) *Plays: 9 (Innocence, The Balancing Act, Tune, A Window, The Edge)* (London: Methuen Drama).

—— (2012a) *The Chair Plays (Have I None, The Under Room, Chair)* (London: Methuen Drama).

—— (2012b) 'I Want to Set Light to People's Souls', Video Interview, *The Guardian*, 24 February, www.guardian.co.uk/stage/video/2012/feb/24edward-bond-video-interview.

Browne, T. (1975) *Playwrights' Theatre: The English Stage Company at the Royal Court* (London: Pitman).

Costa, M. (2011) 'Edward Bond's *Saved*: "We Didn't Set Out to Shock"', *The Guardian*, 9 October, www.guardian.co.uk/stage/2011/oct/09/edward-bond-saved-original-cast.

Coult, T. (1977) *The Plays of Edward Bond* (London: Eyre Methuen).

Davis, D. (ed.) (2005) *Edward Bond and the Dramatic Child: Edward Bond's Plays for Young People* (Stoke on Trent: Trentham Books).

Eagleton, T. (1984) 'Nature and Violence: The Prefaces of Edward Bond', *Critical Quarterly*, 26:1/2, 127–35.

Eagleton, T. and D. Milne (eds) (1996) *Marxist Literary Theory* (Oxford: Blackwell).

Eaves, M. (ed.) (2003) *The Cambridge Companion to William Blake* (Cambridge University Press).

Esslin, M. (1968) Review of *The Sea*, *Plays and Players*, 15 (April), 26.

Euripides (1972) *The Bacchae and Other Plays*, ed. P. Vellacott, 2nd edn (Harmondsworth: Penguin).

Hay, M. and P. Roberts (1980) *Bond: A Study of His Plays* (London: Eyre Methuen).

Hirst, D. L. (1985) *Edward Bond* (London: Macmillan).

Hunka, G. (2007) 'Why Are Some Playwrights Far More Popular Overseas?' Theatre Blog with Lyn Gardner, *The Guardian*, 13 November, www.guardian.co.uk/stage/theatreblog/2007/nov/13/ofthefiveworksin#start-of-comments.

Koppen, U. (1997) Interview with Edward Bond: 'Modern and Postmodern Theatres', *New Theatre Quarterly*, 13, 99–105.

Kuhn, T. and S. Giles (eds) (2003) *Brecht on Art and Politics* (London: Methuen).

Lacey, S. (1995) *British Realist Theatre* (London: Routledge).

Lambley, D. (1992) 'In Search of a Radical Discourse for Theatre', *New Theatre Quarterly*, 8, 34–47.

Lane, D. (2010) *Contemporary British Drama* (Edinburgh University Press).

Logan, B. (2000) 'Still Bolshie After All These Years', *The Guardian*, 5 April, www.guardian.co.uk/culture/2000/apr/05/artsfeatures2.

Mangan, M. (1998) *Edward Bond* (Plymouth: Northcote House).

Massai, S. (1999) 'Stage over Study: Charles Marowitz, Edward Bond, and Recent Materialist Approaches to Shakespeare', *New Theatre Quarterly*, 15:59, 247–55.

Nicholson, H. (2009) *Theatre and Education* (Basingstoke: Palgrave Macmillan).

Pajaczkowska, C. (2000) *Ideas in Psychoanalysis: Perversion* (Cambridge: Icon Books).

Ravenhill, M. (2006) 'Acid Tongue' [an article about Edward Bond], *The Guardian*, 9 September, www.guardian.co.uk/stage/2006/sep/09theatre.stage.

Reinelt, J. (1996) *After Brecht: British Epic Theatre* (Ann Arbor: University of Michigan Press).

Roberts, P. (ed.) (1985) *Bond on File* (London: Methuen).

—— (1999) *The Royal Court Theatre and the Modern Stage* (Cambridge University Press).

Saunders, G. (2004) 'Edward Bond and the Celebrity of Exile', *Theatre Research International*, 29:3, 256–66.

Scharine, R. (1976) *The Plays of Edward Bond* (London: Associated University Presses).

Spencer, J. S. (1992) *Dramatic Strategies in the Plays of Edward Bond* (Cambridge University Press).

Stuart, I. (1994) 'A Political Language for the Theatre: Edward Bond's RSC Workshops, 1992', *New Theatre Quarterly*, 10:39, 207–16.

—— (1996) *Politics in Performance: The Production Work of Edward Bond, 1978–1990* (London: Peter Lang).

Taylor, J. Russell (1970) 'British Dramatists: The New Arrivals, no. 5: Edward Bond', *Plays and Players*, 17 (August), 16–18.

Trussler, S. (1976) *Edward Bond* (Harlow: Longman).

Want, C. and A. Klimowski (2011) *Introducing Kant* (London: Icon Books).

Wheen, F. (2006) *Marx's Das Kapital: A Biography* (London: Atlantic Books).

Index

Figures are shown in **bold**.

Printed and bound in Great Britain by
CPI Group (UK) Ltd, Croydon, CR0 4YY